W9-BKO-583

Almost every conceivable problem we run into today can be traced to a breakdown in our relationships. We need help and we need a guide, and Debra is that. This book is an amazing tool that can bring healing, joy, and depth at so many levels! I know it did for me.

Jefferson Bethke, *New York Times* bestselling author of *Jesus >Religion* and *To Hell with the Hustle*

Love in Every Season expertly uncovers the challenge and promise of every season of love and marriage. It offers hope, perspective, encouragement, and instruction for every romantic relationship at every stage. Highly recommended.

Gary Thomas, author of *Sacred Marriage* and *Cherish*

Love in Every Season has the page-turning entertainment of the best fiction, but with rich, hard-hitting truths, practical principles, inspirational true stories, and even some great comic relief sprinkled into every chapter. As readers, we felt invited on a journey while also being impacted with biblical truths and timeless tools to help our own marriage. This book is destined to become a masterpiece among marriage and relationship books.

Dave and Ashley Willis, authors of *The Naked Marriage* and hosts of The Naked Marriage podcast

Love in Every Season will transform the way you look at love. Debra will take you on a captivating ride through the four seasons of love with a new perspective and practical advice that you can apply today. Whether you're single, dating, or married, you'll discover what it takes to truly make love grow through every age and stage.

Drs. Les and Leslie Parrott, #1 *New York Times* bestselling authors of *Saving Your Marriage Before It Starts*

No matter your relationship status, this book is for you. This book is pivotal to helping you become the mother, husband, daughter, father, or mother-in-law God intended you to be.

Levi Lusko, lead pastor of Fresh Life Church and bestselling author

Debra is one of the most insightful voices on relationships today, and whether you've been married for 30 years or dating for only a few months, you will love this book. *Love in Every Season* is compelling and filled with wisdom that explains so much about how to navigate the inevitable "seasons" of life and relationship.

Shaunti Feldhahn, social researcher and bestselling author of *For Women Only* and *The Surprising Secrets of Highly Happy Marriages*

Debra Fileta is a talented speaker, trusted counselor, and an amazing writer. *Love in Every Season* is the perfect book for your relationships, whether your love is just blooming or you are struggling with the winter blues. Engaging and impactful, Debra's insights are the remedy needed for those who desire authentic intimacy, biblical insights, and practical ways to grow healthy relationships.

Dr. Chris and Alisa Grace, Center for Marriage and Relationships, Biola University

Debra's words of wisdom will inspire and instruct you toward the health and success of a current relationship or any future relationships. *Love in Every Season* reads as if you were sitting across from Debra in a comfortable chair, sipping tea, and soaking in her encouraging and hope-filled observations. Get this book and make Debra your personal relationship mentor!

Chris Reed, pastor at Saddleback Church

LOVE

IN EVERY SEASON

DEBRA FILETA
M.A., LPC

HARVEST HOUSE PUBLISHERS
EUGENE, OREGON

Cover design by Kara Klontz Design

Cover Photo © Irtsya, Elmiral, Geo Module / Shutterstock

Published in association with the literary agency of D.C. Jacobson & Associates LLC, an Author Management Company. www.dcjacobson.com..

This book contains stories in which the author has changed people's names and some details of their situations in order to protect their privacy.

Love in Every Season
Copyright © 2019 by Debra Fileta
Published by Harvest House Publishers
Eugene, Oregon 97408
www.harvesthousepublishers.com

ISBN 978-0-7369-7759-3 (pbk.)
ISBN 978-0-7369-7760-9 (eBook)

Library of Congress Cataloging-in-Publication Data

Names: Fileta, Debra K. author.
Title: Love in every season / Debra Fileta, M.A., LPC.
Description: Eugene : Harvest House Publishers, 2020.
Identifiers: LCCN 2019027328 (print) | LCCN 2019027329 (ebook) | ISBN
    9780736977593 (trade paperback) | ISBN 9780736977609 (ebook)
Subjects: LCSH: Interpersonal relations—Religious aspects—Christianity. |
    Love—Religious aspects—Christianity—Anecdotes. |
    Seasons—Miscellanea.
Classification: LCC BV4597.52 .F55 2020 (print) | LCC BV4597.52 (ebook) |
    DDC 241/.676—dc23
LC record available at https://lccn.loc.gov/2019027328
LC ebook record available at https://lccn.loc.gov/2019027329

To the four greatest loves of my life: my husband, John, and our Ella, Eli, and Ezzy.

It is my honor and privilege to be able to love and serve you. May God give us the wisdom and the courage to always pursue love in every season.

CONTENTS

INTRODUCTION

My husband and I spent one year of our marriage in Florida. After finishing up his medical residency, John decided to pursue specialized training. Since this fellowship would take one year to complete, we determined there was no better place to live for a year than in the Sunshine State. So, we packed up all our belongings in a 6' x 12' mobile storage unit, loaded up the kids, and caught a train down to Florida.

The best part about living in Florida is that it feels like you are perpetually on vacation. Every day is perfectly sunny and warm, palm trees greet you every single morning, and the beautiful, sandy beach is just minutes away. It is a tropical slice of paradise.

Because we moved to Florida from the East Coast, we noticed something about this new domain very quickly: *There were no seasons.* The temperature just went from hot, to hotter, to excruciatingly hot, and back to hotter again. There was no such thing as the changing of the weather from one month to another. Day after day, everything looked and felt pretty much the same.

In the beginning of our time in Florida, this lack of variety in the weather felt incredible. Who needs seasons when every single day is sunny and warm, with the salty sea breeze blowing against your face? It was perfect. And we were going to enjoy every minute of it! But right around October, things started to get weird. My pumpkin spice latte just didn't feel the same stepping out into 94-degree weather, with a wave of hot air blowing against my face. I found myself missing the changing of the temperature, my fall wardrobe, and the beautiful colors of autumn.

By December, this permanent state of hot and sunny was starting to feel redundant. Turning on the radio to "Let It Snow! Let It Snow! Let It Snow!"while we were driving to the beach felt like a big joke. Putting up our Christmas tree and then stringing the lights outside in shorts and a T-shirt didn't feel as festive as usual. We were trying to convince ourselves that Christmas was coming, but it felt more like the Fourth of July.

Don't get me wrong—Floridians really do try their best to mimic the seasons. They get their boots, hats, and gloves on when it is 78 degrees outside on a "brisk night." They decorate for Christmas with more lights, reindeer, and blow-up snowmen than anywhere I've ever seen. They even have snow machines blowing snowflake-like soapsuds from the palm treetops all through December. They really do try. But at the end of the day, there's no replicating the awe-inspiring experience of passing through the seasons.

The Four Seasons

Spring, summer, fall, winter. The four seasons signify the passing of one year. Every one of those seasons holds a special place in my heart. Each one of those seasons possesses unique beauty, weather patterns, and natural quirks. One of my favorite things to do is sit at my kitchen table and look out over our backyard through the large-paneled window that faces our deck. Our neighborhood is built in a valley, so when you look outside, you see the high, rolling hills of Pennsylvania all around. Watching the seasons change from that vantage point is breathtaking. For the past few years that we've lived in this home, I've been deliberate about taking a photo of that picturesque view with the passing of each season because each season comes with its own picture, plan, and purpose.

In spring, the trees are blooming with the most incredible shades and varieties of pink, magenta, and white blossoms. In summer, the vibrant leaves clothe the tree branches with a new coat of greenery. In fall, the air becomes crisp, and the sun glimmers past yellow, orange, and red leaves like through a stained-glass window. And then winter comes, with its calming blanket of white, powdery snow covering everything in sight. The bare branches glisten in the sun, carrying the weight of snow and ice.

Each season in nature is unique and necessary. Each season has a role and a reason. Each season adds its own unique layer, building the foundation as it ushers in the season to come.

The Four Seasons of a Relationship

Have you ever heard someone talk about "how naturally" their romantic relationship progressed? "Naturally" conveys the idea that something is happening *as in nature*—without being controlled, manipulated, or forced to happen. It unfolds in an expected and predictable way.

As a professional counselor and relationship specialist, I get an eye-opening, front-row seat into the lives and relationships of many individuals and couples. One thing I have witnessed is that all relationships pass through a predictable pattern of interactions that I like to call the "seasons" of a relationship: spring, summer, fall, and winter. These four seasons of a relationship mimic the seasons we pass through in nature. Just as nature passes through the four seasons, so do relationships. There's an expected pattern of seasons that every healthy relationship will go through as it develops and grows. The seasons don't always happen in order. They can take months to unfold in a relationship or even years. And often, a relationship will cycle through these seasons again and again. But their presence is always sure and their purpose clear.

> There's an expected pattern of seasons
> that every healthy relationship will go
> through as it develops and grows.

Spring is a time of new beginnings. In spring, emotions are in full bloom. Everything about the relationship seems bright and beautiful.

Attraction is growing at a very rapid pace. Spring is a time of planting good seeds in a relationship and a time of uprooting any harmful weeds, and we have to know exactly what we're looking for in order for our relationship to succeed.

The season of summer in a relationship is when things start to get hot. The heat of summer causes us to begin shedding our layers, getting to know one another in a deeper and more deliberate way. We start experiencing the warmth of emotional intimacy, the heat of physical intimacy, and the fire of spiritual intimacy, and we've got to learn how to navigate each of those areas in a healthy and meaningful way so that we don't get burned.

The season of fall is when our true colors begin to shine in the relationship. We're no longer blinded by the brightness and beauty of spring because in fall we begin to see things as they really are. The cover we once had begins to fall, and we realize we've got nowhere to hide from our flaws and weaknesses. It's a season of deep connection and communication, and we either learn to embrace the vulnerability and authenticity of this season, or our relationship gets stuck.

Then there's the season of winter: the time when things begin to cool as the normalcy of day-to-day life sets in. Winter offers us an opportunity to lean in to the comfort and stability of familiarity, but it also sets us up for the dangerous frost of apathy and the freezing of intentionality. We can start getting so accustomed to love that we begin to take it for granted. If we approach winter with understanding, we can allow our relationship to be strengthened by the struggle; otherwise, we allow the struggle to sever our relationship.

Each of these four seasons is an important part of creating and maintaining a healthy relationship. Even Solomon, one of the wisest people to walk the earth, understood that for everything in life there are seasons. In Ecclesiastes 3:1, he reminds us, "There is a time for everything, and a season for every activity under the heavens." God instilled creation with a beautiful order, and our relationships are yet another avenue in which we get to see His creativity, wisdom, and majesty unfold.

Each season of a relationship is unique and necessary, revealing both the strengths and weaknesses of the relationship. Each season comes with its own plan and purpose, offering opportunities for growth and intimacy. Some seasons come with difficulty. Others are filled with joy. But each season plays a specific role in determining the health and well-being of a relationship. Oftentimes, these seasons happen one by one, and as one season finishes, a couple finds themselves moving into the next one. But other times, these seasons happen simultaneously, throughout the life of a relationship. Because each couple is made up of unique people with unique needs, a season can unfold in just a few months, or it can take years. Yet, no matter how these seasons unfold, it is up to us to see them as an invitation, an opportunity to draw deeper and to grow closer to one another.

So often, people pass through these four seasons of a relationship without ever recognizing them for what they are. They move through the stages of a relationship without any awareness. They face the elements of the seasons without being prepared, forfeiting the opportunity for growth, maturity, and intimacy. If you don't recognize the seasons, you'll never be able to learn from them.

> If you don't recognize the seasons, you'll
> never be able to learn from them.

Love in Every Season

No matter what your age or stage of relationship—single, dating, or married—you will face relationships that challenge you to grow and mature. Relationships expose our level of emotional and spiritual health, as well as the health—or lack thereof—of our personal interactions. In all your closest relationships—whether it be your marriage, a dating relationship, a friendship, or even with family—recognizing the season you're in and then seeing it as a purposeful experience is critical to achieving a healthy relationship. Are you ready to open your heart to receive all that love has to offer? For those who are willing and ready, there is an opportunity to find love in every season.

Section 1:

SPRING—NEW LIFE AND NEW LOVE

Spring is the season of new beginnings.

It's a time of new life, new growth, and new experiences. It's a bright and beautiful season filled with the budding of interest and the blossoming of attraction. In this joyful season, the sun is shining brightly, and everything is seen through a filter of beauty.

Spring is also a time for planting. It's the season of sowing the seeds of a relationship, understanding that whatever we sow during this season will eventually take root. It's a time of being intentional to cultivate the faith and friendship we want to grow, while being deliberate to remove the weeds that might be harming our relationship. It's also a time of pruning, of trimming back the excess—of learning to let go of the things that are holding us back and stretching out our branches toward new heights of growth.

Spring is a magnificent season, and it's one that every healthy relationship must learn how to pass through with intentionality. The seeds of spring will eventually take root and one day bear fruit that will impact every other season of a relationship.

1

SPRING IS IN THE AIR— PLANTING GOOD SEEDS

t wasn't love at first sight. Not for me, anyway. When I met John for the first time, there were no bells or whistles, no butterflies in my stomach or palpitations in my chest, no voices from heaven or spotlight in the clouds shining down, no "signs" like we are typically told there will be when we meet the person with whom we will spend the rest of our lives. In reality, I wasn't even thinking of love at the time—at least, not love toward him.

I met John at a conference in Boston—one that I had hesitantly agreed to attend, and when he walked in the room, the first thing I thought to myself was, *Wow, that guy is tall,* followed by an extremely deep observation: *Who wears a pair of shorts coupled with a long-sleeve dress shirt?* And that's pretty much it. After the seminar was over each day, about 30 of us would spend the rest of the day mingling. It was a group in which we both had mutual friends. One day we all went mini golfing. The next day, we took a road trip to the beach. Each day, we somehow continued to end up in the same group, the same car, or on the same team. So, naturally, we had some time to get to know each other. And slowly but surely, I found the seeds of friendship beginning to take root in our interactions.

A few days into the conference, my friend pointed out our budding friendship, and I remember telling her, "He's the nicest guy I've ever met…but there's about a 0.0000000001 percent chance I'd marry someone like him." I wasn't really interested in getting into a relationship at that point in my life because a few months before that, I'd had my heart truly broken in a relationship with a guy who wasn't as into me as I was into him. My heart was in hibernation mode—I wasn't ready to hope again. Added to that, I was in the thick of graduate school *and* we lived thousands of miles apart. There were so many reasons to write off the idea of building a relationship. Yet, watching him interact with others, seeing his heart for Jesus, and listening to his absolutely hilarious stories made me want to be his friend. Little did I know then that this was the first step in building a relationship that would lead to a friendship, that would lead to a marriage, that would lead to the rest of my life. The seeds we planted in friendship would ultimately reap a harvest in our future marriage—a flourishing marriage more deep, intimate, and meaningful than I could have ever imagined.

On the Other Hand

John says he knew I was the girl he was going to marry just a few moments after we met. Everything inside of him "just knew." It is not surprising, I suppose, considering he is the romantic one in our relationship. Even so, it seemed to go against everything he knew and believed about relationships to feel so strongly, so soon. The evening we met he called his best friend to help him debrief these strange feelings he was having:

"So, I think I met the woman I'm going to marry," he said.

"John, you're crazy," his friend confirmed on the other end of the line and tried snapping him back to reality.

Maybe he *was* crazy, but something about our interactions seemed different to him. Something about our new friendship made him want to invest in getting to know me and see where our relationship would go.

When people ask us how we met, I love to listen to him tell his side of the story and compare all the differences between the thoughts and feelings we each had going into our relationship. But no matter how different our stories may sound at the outset, the next steps we had to take were the same: In order for us to know if this relationship was built to last, we first had to navigate through the four seasons of a relationship.

> But no matter how different our stories may sound at the outset, the next steps we had to take were the same: In order for us to know if this relationship was built to last, we first had to navigate through the four seasons of a relationship.

A Season for Everything

"When you met your husband, did you get a confirmation?"

I had just finished speaking to a group of 20- and 30-year-olds at a church in central Pennsylvania, when one of the young ladies came up to me with this very interesting question.

"Confirmation?" I asked, somewhat puzzled. "What do you mean?"

"From God. A confirmation from God," she specified, surprised that I even needed clarification.

How unspiritual of me, I chuckled to myself, knowing that the only two things running through my mind at the word "confirmation" were my airline tickets and that class my Catholic friends had to take as kids to become part of their church.

"Umm, no," I replied casually.

I could tell by the look on her face that this was not the answer she wanted. So, it was my turn to clarify. I explained that when I met my husband, nothing told me I'd met the man I was going to marry. Our relationship didn't start as a one-time decision; it was a process—a process that was "confirmed" to me one step at a time by the interactions we had in each stage of our relationship.

The question presented by this sweet, well-intentioned young woman illustrates a problem with what we are taught in church culture about finding a lifelong relationship. We tend to view the process of choosing a partner as a one-time revelation, a feeling, a thought, an experience, an interaction, or even a spotlight from heaven that screams, "Yes! This is the one you should marry!"

While such revelations do happen for some people sometimes, most of the Christian life doesn't happen in one-time magical moments, but in the process of our day-to-day lives. Relationships are quite the same because great relationships take time to unfold, to take shape, and to grow into nourishing interactions that set the stage for a thriving, God-honoring marriage. With good intentions, we tend to overspiritualize love as a miraculous moment rather than seeing love as a series of seasons and stages. Just as in nature, love unfolds season by season—beginning with spring.

> Most of the Christian life doesn't happen
> in one-time magical moments, but in
> the process of our day-to-day lives.

Spring Is in the Air

Spring comes in the Northern Hemisphere when the earth tilts back toward the sun, allowing for more sunlight and warmth to cover God's creation. It is the time of new life, new growth, and new experiences. The warmth of the sun awakens the plants and trees from hibernation, and new life begins to "spring forth," breaking the ground with excitement and anticipation. It is a beautiful time of year as flowers are in full bloom, showing off their vibrant colors and sweet aromas. Spring is a time for a fresh start. It is a time for something new.

The season of spring in a relationship is also a time for new things. New feelings begin to bloom, calling our hearts out from hibernation. It is a time of awakening from the hibernation of sadness, of heartbreak, or of loneliness, and coming into the newness of love, healing, and relationships.

Spring is such an important first stage for a relationship to pass through because it is a time of rapid growth. It is always accompanied by strong feelings of attraction and an anticipation for what's to come. Spring is a time when feelings might even be exaggerated since the relationship is viewed through a rose-colored lens.

I don't know about you, but I can personally relate to the idea of exaggerated feelings and wearing a rose-colored lens. A few months before our wedding, John and I were in premarital counseling in anticipation of the big day. The counselor asked us to take a compatibility inventory to get a sense of our respective feelings about each other and our relationship. Part of the inventory was to rate our personal level of satisfaction in the relationship as well as point out any issues or problem spots we were seeing in our partner. I'll never forget my rose-colored lens as I quickly and confidently gave our relationship the highest scores possible in every category. Every single aspect of it was "amazing," and John was pretty much perfect in my eyes. Looking back, it astonishes me how easy it was for me to see everything through the lens of spring. But even with my exaggerated perspective, the seeds I was seeing in spring were truly seeds that would last with us for a lifetime. After over a decade of marriage, I have to admit that my rose-colored lens is much more realistic today; yet even so, I clearly see the good seeds that were planted in spring evidenced in our marriage each day.

In spring, the seeds you plant begin to take root, shaping the landscape of how the relationship will look. What you see in spring will likely be evident in every season of the relationship. So, it is important to learn to plant the right seeds and recognize and remove the weeds.

You Reap What You Sow

Whether you are in the season of spring as a dating couple or as a married couple, you need to remember that the seeds you plant in the beginning of your relationship, when the soil is most fertile, are the seeds that will grow and bear fruit throughout the rest of your relationship. The seeds you plant have a direct impact on the health of your relationship. Scripture affirms this general principle: "The seed whose fruit is righteousness is sown in peace by those who make peace" (James 3:18 NASB). Again, Galatians 6:7 reminds us, "Whatever a man sows... he will also reap" (NASB).

Spring is a time of planting, a time of being deliberate and intentional about the things that will eventually take root and ultimately become the entire landscape of your relationship. When it comes to planting and sowing, there are two important components that can't be overlooked in spring: the seeds of faith and the seeds of friendship.

The Seeds of Faith

In Matthew 17, we find a story of faith. In this passage, a father whose son is in desperate need of healing approaches Jesus. The father kneels before Him, asking for mercy for his son, who is struggling with severe spiritual and physical ailments. Jesus lays hands on this boy, and in an instant, the boy receives freedom in his spirit and healing in his body. Then, Jesus turns to His disciples and quotes one of the most familiar passages of Scripture, "If you have faith like a grain of mustard seed, you will say to this mountain, 'Move from here to there,' and it will move, and nothing will be impossible for you" (Matthew 17:20 ESV).

In reading this passage, the concept that stuck out to me more than anything is that faith like a grain of mustard seed means faith that grows. It may start small, but in order for a mustard seed to have an impact, it has to be planted and tended to. Warren Wiersbe puts it this way:

> "Faith as a grain of mustard seed" suggests not only size (God will honor even a little faith), but also *life* and *growth*. Faith like a mustard seed is a *living* faith that is nurtured and caused to grow. Faith must be cultivated so that it grows and does even greater exploits for God (1 Thessalonians 3:10; 2 Thessalonians 1:3).[1]

In order for us to have healthy relationships, our faith in Jesus and the work He is doing in our lives is the most important seed in our life. We must pay attention to it, cultivate it, and nurture it so that it grows, inviting God's supernatural work inside of us and impacting everyone around us. For the hope of healthy relationships, the seed of faith must be the most important element in our life.

If you are married, throughout every season and stage of a relationship, it is important to ask yourself what types of seeds you are planting in your relationship, and what kind of fruit is being produced as a result. Are you investing in your relationship with Jesus and allowing Him to cultivate and produce good traits in your life? Are you planting seeds of faith, of hope, of encouragement, of peace? Or are you planting seeds of bitterness, criticism, complaint, and discouragement? Learning to cultivate the right seeds—the seeds of faith—in your personal life and in your relationships is something we will talk about in more detail as we get deeper into the concepts of this book.

If you are single, faith must be a primary ingredient in your life as well as in your romantic relationships. Your relationship will only be as healthy as you are standing alone. When you start dating, keep in mind that what you see in dating, you'll also see in marriage. If, in the season of spring, you are not seeing the seeds of faith alive and active in the life of someone you are dating, you have to ask yourself what kind of fruit you expect to see in a few years. In nature, good fruit doesn't just magically appear on its own; it has to be planted and tended. The same is true of our relationships. In order for you to experience the "good fruit" of healthy relationships, you have to be planting the seeds of faith in your life and in your relationships.

> Your relationship will only be as
> healthy as you are standing alone.

Got Fruit?

Meeting John felt different from meeting any other guy, the primary reason being that his character stood out above anything else. I watched as he interacted with others with kindness and love. I saw him serving others in many different ways and going out of his way to show love to those around him. I was struck by his sense of humor and his desire to make others laugh. I also noted his humility, how he always chose to ask questions first instead of talking about himself. He had a distinct character that exuded from him to everyone he interacted with. Meeting him was different because it wasn't chemistry but *character* that led the way for our relationship to begin taking root.

I'll be the first to admit that in my past, I was typically drawn to men based on their appearance, and naively, I had a pretty narrow preference: blond haired, blue-eyed guys with a medium height and build, and artistic or musical tendencies. John was a good-looking guy, but the complete opposite of my cookie-cutter preferences: dark hair, dark eyes, extremely tall, with no artistic tendencies whatsoever, and not a musical bone in his body. Yet, slowly and consistently, my attraction to him grew and developed in a remarkable way. The chemistry began to catch up with the character as I got to know him from the "inside out," observing the seeds of faith in his life.

I saw the Spirit's work displayed in John's life: "But the fruit of the Spirit is love, joy, peace, forbearance, kindness, goodness, faithfulness, gentleness and self-control" (Galatians 5:22-23). If you want to see good fruit in your relationships, you have to start with good seeds. Seeds will eventually become fruit, which is why this concept is so important to grasp in the season of spring. So much of the future success of a relationship hinges on this concept of sowing good seeds. The Bible reminds us that those who sow seeds of the Spirit, will reap the Spirit's reward of eternal life, but those who sow seeds of the flesh will reap destruction (Galatians 6:8).

> If you want to see good fruit in your relationships,
> you have to start with good seeds.

What types of seeds are you sowing in your life and in your relationships?

The Seeds of Friendship

You can learn a lot about a person in the early stages of friendship, and certainly enough to tell you whether or not this relationship is worth taking the next step. Friendship is the most underestimated component of a relationship, but it is at the core of every meaningful relationship we have. Friendship connects people with shared interests, beliefs, experiences, qualities, and goals. Friendship is the coming together of two people who like each other and want to spend time together, who value and respect one another, and who have chosen to be together just because they want to be. Friendship gives people an opportunity to get to know what a person is made of when there are no strings of commitment attached. It provides a chance to get a good glimpse of what the future might hold.

Something I notice in working with clients in troubled romantic relationships is that many of them rushed into romantic relationships, skipping right over the friendship stage. They let romance lead the way in their relationship, but when the fires of romance began to wane, they had nothing left to sustain them because there was no friendship in the first place. I find it ironic that many people today giving relationship advice actually encourage people to *avoid* crossing the lines of friendship into dating. "You'll get friend-zoned," they tell you. "Don't ruin your friendship by dating," they warn. We live in a society that tends to value feelings over friendship —"Why be friends, when you can be lovers?" But the real question we should be asking is, "How can you be lovers without being friends?" Friendship is the relationship that will sustain you through the seasons of love. Some of the most incredible marriages I have witnessed are built between people who share a deep and lasting friendship. While romance may come and go throughout the life of a relationship, friendship always remains constant.

How can you be lovers without being friends?

The seeds of a relationship show up pretty quickly in the friendship stage. And they can teach you a lot if you know where to look. Even while John and I were in these extremely early stages of a friendship, the seeds of our relationship were quickly being exposed and coming to the surface.

Friends Before Lovers

I saw a funny picture the other day that said, "A good friend is like a good bra: hard to find, supportive, comfortable, always lifts you up, makes you look better, and is close to your heart." Okay, so maybe there are better analogies out there, but it is true that great friendships are hard to come by! The ingredients in a friendship are the exact components that you will bring into a romantic relationship, so it is great to have an idea of what you'll be building upon before your heart gets romantically involved.

When John and I met, our feelings may have been at different stages, but we both took the next natural step into friendship. In fact, our friendship progressed for five months and paved the way for us to move into a dating relationship. It was a great time of getting to know each other in a low-pressure environment, surrounded by our closest friends.

Because relationships are all so different, there are no hard-and-fast rules, but when asked, I always suggest a period of friendship of at least three months before you decide to take the next steps into a dating relationship. Here are some reasons why friendship builds a solid foundation for a romantic relationship.

Friendship teaches you what you need to know. Have you ever known a couple where just being around them gives you all the vibes that they are a great match? My friends Luke and Christy are one of those couples. They are such a great match because they really took their time to learn what they needed to know in their stage of friendship. They met in a ministry that they were both a part of, and with time, it was clear that their personalities really meshed. They had so much in common, and their differences just fit together so well.

But the main reason they figured out they were a good match is the time they spent together during friendship. Their singles community was a true community, so they had a lot of time to get to know one another as friends. They ate meals together, went to church together, served together, and hung out together. They spent a lot of their free time together in the context of their singles group with a range of activities including bowling, football games, ice-cream socials, and ministry opportunities. It was in the context of these many interactions that they developed a deep friendship and got to know each other in a significant way. When you spend a lot of time with friends, you get to know everyone's quirks, see their different personalities, and get a really good sense of who you connect with and who you don't.

One of my favorite things about the stage of friendship that precedes a romantic relationship is that it gives you a chance to get a good idea of the person you are getting to know, before the cloud of romanticism gets in the way. It is the perfect opportunity to learn so many crucial things about a person, eliminating the element of surprise and decreasing the risk of heartbreak. Friendship is an opportunity to get a glimpse of a person's personality, spiritual life, hobbies and interests, communication skills, and social abilities without the pressure of commitment getting in the way.

Friendship offers a low-pressure environment. John and I developed a strong friendship through games of miniature golf, candlepin bowling, city exploration, and restaurant hopping. It was the no-pressure zone in which we began letting down our guard and testing the waters of compatibility. We had so much in common and genuinely enjoyed each other's company. Spending time in nonromantic settings and with groups of other friends were some of the most crucial moments in building this deep friendship that we still have today. We made each other laugh, encouraged each other, and had so much fun together long before the seeds of romance had been planted in our hearts (well, at least long before we had spoken them out loud!). When we started developing our friendship, we were almost always surrounded by people we loved and got an incredible glimpse into each other's lives and communities. Not only that, but the atmosphere of friendship gave us the opportunity to get to know each other without adding any physical affection to skew our emotions one way or the other.

The beauty about genuine friendship is that it tends to progress naturally. Oftentimes, a friendship will start in some sort of a social environment (church, work, school, sports, ministry, etc.), and as the friendship grows, it slowly progresses into a one-on-one relationship. The best romantic relationships are discovered when we approach them like we do all other friendships—as opportunities to invest in the people that God has placed in our lives, while allowing them to invest in us. Get involved in the community that God has placed you in. If you are not involved in a community of people, ask God to lead you into a small group, a church environment, a service-based project, or even a social group, and get plugged in!

If you are single and looking, be deliberate about investing in a group of friends—even if that means stepping out of your comfort zone—and then watch and see what God begins to do within those natural relationships. Where we make the greatest mistake, and where hearts are most broken and confused, is when we prematurely take a relationship out of the safety of community and into the exclusivity of a romantic situation. Take off the pressure and get to know the people around you. You never know what might happen next.

Friendship has roots that run deep into marriage. One Christmas, our kids got a ball pit that we set up in their downstairs playroom. While they were playing in their ball pit one evening, I got the mischievous idea to crawl in with them and start chucking the soft plastic balls at my unsuspecting husband. What started as a playful gesture turned into a hilarious ball-throwing battle; we laughed so hard that I think I may have peed my pants—just a little.

Our kids had a blast, but most importantly, they got to see that beyond the role of "mom" and "dad," their parents are really, truly friends. The roots that began in our friendship run deep, and to this day our friendship continues to fuel much of our love for one another.

From a hot date night to sitting at home watching reruns and folding laundry or laughing until our sides hurt, life together is fun—not because of what we are doing, but because of the friendship that we have. There's no friend on earth with whom I'd rather spend time, and John says the same about me. And that's a good thing because we get to be together for the rest of our lives. Ultimately, investing in friendship sets the stage for the four seasons of a relationship.

Finding Friendship Again

As a professional counselor, I find that many relationships may start with the right seeds but get caught up in the demands and distractions of life. In Matthew 13, Jesus tells a parable of a man who sowed good seeds—but his seeds fell into thorns, were choked out, and died. In this story, the seeds represent the seed of the Word of God, and the thorns represent the worries and demands of this world that choke out our ability to absorb God's truth. But I think the same concept can apply to our relationships and marriages. If we're not careful, there are so many thorns in this life that can choke out our good seeds—the stresses of work, extended family, raising a family, finances, and even physical and emotional health. Life is filled with so many distractions that can keep us from cultivating and nurturing the good seeds of our relationship.

For us, that distraction came with having children. We love our children, value the blessing and joy they bring into our lives, and wouldn't trade them for anything in the world, but if we're not careful, they can also suck the life out of our relationship. We quickly found out how difficult it can be to connect when all our energy was focused on them. From the baby stage of wiping, and feeding, and changing, and walking around like zombies because we have hardly gotten a wink of sleep in months, to the later stages of school, and schedules, and sports, and activities, and emotions, and conversations—we can find that the seeds of our love start getting choked out by life's demands. But it doesn't have to be that way. It is important to nurture our relationship no matter what season of life we're in, taking the time to intentionally connect with one another and rekindle that deep friendship, even if that means saying "no" to things in our schedule so that we can say "yes" to one another.

For me and John, that means we take time to invest in our friendship. We love reading books together, watching movies together, and playing board games together. We love window shopping, traveling, drinking coffee, going to the beach, and trying new restaurants. We make it a point to get away by ourselves a couple times a year to enjoy the things we love, rekindle our friendship, and invest in having fun.

Find the things you have in common and make it a point to connect on those things. If you don't feel like you have much in common, find something new that you can do together. Read books together. Join an activity together. Get involved in a hobby together. The key is prioritizing togetherness when everything in this culture might be pushing you toward isolation and aloneness. We live in a "you do you" world that tells us that the road to happiness is found when you can do what you want, when you want, how you want. But God's way gently reminds us that the road to happiness begins when we can learn to put the needs and wants of others before ourselves, when we can delight in their joy as our own (Philippians 2:3). It's not about *me*; it's about *we*.

I know a couple who took up bicycling (even though neither of them was previously interested in it) in order to find something to do together. It became such a point of connection and friendship for them and took their relationship to a new level. Take the time to remember what it feels like to have fun in your relationship, and be deliberate about planning outings and activities where you can rekindle your friendship and enjoy one another's company.

The Sow-Sow Relationship

You may be reading this chapter as a married person and nodding your head in agreement at the importance of developing a friendship and the gift that it is to be best friends in marriage. But you may also be married and find yourself reading this section with a hint of disappointment and regret because your relationship is more of a "so-so" relationship, and you lack that sense of being married to your best friend. Maybe you rushed into a relationship and didn't really take the time to see the seeds of friendship grow before it was too late. Or maybe you are grieving the realization that your spouse is not anywhere close to your best friend, and you are struggling with feelings of bitterness and disappointment. If that is where you find yourself today, I want to encourage you and offer you hope that seeds can *always* be planted in marriage.

If you find yourself struggling in a so-so relationship, there's no better time to sow, sow, sow! Start planting good seeds right now, starting today. The moment you decide you want to commit to doing things differently is the moment you breathe hope and life into your future. The fact that you are reading this book tells me that you desire to have a healthy marriage. The choices you make today are going to bear fruit eventually. It may not happen right away. No seed bears fruit overnight. But in time, the seeds you plant will have an impact.[2]

If you find yourself struggling in a so-so relationship,
there's no better time to sow, sow, sow!

When you learn to value yourself, understand your identity in Christ, recognize your limits, confess your sins, set boundaries, work on your weaknesses, increase your strengths, communicate your needs, and pursue healthy conflict, you begin to plant seeds of life and love in your marriage. Find yourself a Christian licensed counselor and get started on the process of healing. Your one and only job is to get yourself healthy, and then trust God with the other half of the equation, asking Him to do that same work in the life of your spouse.

Spring is a season of planting, a season of sowing. It is a time of filling our life and our relationship with the good seeds of both friendship and faith. Spring is an invitation to trust and believe that the God who called us to plant the good seeds will be the God who causes those seeds to grow—both in our life and in our love.

Spring is an invitation to trust and believe
that the God who called us to plant the good
seeds will be the God who causes those seeds
to grow—both in our life and in our love.

Now that we've set the stage for spring with the importance of planting seeds, let's dig a little deeper in this discussion because planting the right seeds is only the first step to making a healthy relationship grow.

Reflection Questions for Couples

1. What "fruits" are we seeing in our relationship, and what type of seeds are we planting?

2. What are some ways I can be deliberate in cultivating "seeds of faith" in my individual life? In my relationship?

3. Did we make time for the seeds of friendship in our relationship?

   a. If yes, what was meaningful about that time? What did we learn about one another during the stage of friendship? What are some of the qualities of our friendship that have carried over into our current relationship?

   b. If no, what are some things that are choking out our friendship? What are some ways that we can cultivate friendship in our relationship? What are some mutual hobbies, activities, and interests we can invest in as a couple?

Reflection Questions for Singles

1. In what ways am I cultivating seeds of faith in my life? What are some steps I can take to nurture and grow that faith?

2. "Where we make the greatest mistake, and where hearts are most broken and confused, is when we prematurely take a relationship out of the safety of community and into the exclusivity of a romantic situation." Reflect on this statement. Have you ever prematurely taken a relationship out of the context of community and into the exclusivity of a romantic relationship? What were the results? How will you do things differently as you move forward?

3. Is there anyone in my current circle of friends that I would like to invest in getting to know more/deepening our friendship?

4. What are the qualities and traits that you would like to see in someone during the friendship stage that would encourage you to pursue a more exclusive dating relationship?

2

WHAT'S BLOOMIN'— THE LAWS OF ATTRACTION

'll never forget the first time we held hands—it was electric.

It was a cold night in November. Both of our arms were resting on that skinny shared armrest between us in the movie theater. At any other time, I probably would have been annoyed that I had to share an armrest. But this time, I was thrilled. It meant I got to be just a little closer to him. And then it happened. All of a sudden, our pinkies were touching. It was the best feeling ever. And if that wasn't enough, within seconds, they were overlapping! And before I knew what had happened, he reached over and gently held my hand. His warm, soft, strong hand was tenderly holding mine, our fingers interlocked in their own embrace.

Okay, I get it—enough with the overly dramatic description. But this, my friends, is exactly the type of thing you should eventually find in the season of spring: *attraction*.

New Life, New Love

The season of spring in a relationship is a time for new things. New feelings begin to bloom, and it is a time of awakening from the hibernation of guardedness, isolation, sadness, heartbreak, or loneliness, and into the newness of love, excitement, anticipation, and connection.

Spring is such an important first stage for a couple to pass through

because it is a time of rapid growth. It is always accompanied by feelings of attraction and an anticipation for what's to come. Feelings in
spring might even be exaggerated because it's hard to see flaws when
the sun is shining so brightly. Caught up in the wave of strong attraction, you're less likely to find things to critique or see traits that need to
be changed. Everything about the relationship is glowing and bright
and beautiful.

In spring, your connection begins moving toward the direction of
a romance. The seeds you planted in friendship are ready to grow into
something more, and the aroma and color of your affection and feelings for one another are out in the open. Spring is a time of anticipation and excitement in a relationship. The "sparks" are flying, and you
find yourself wondering if those sparks have what it takes to turn into a
steady flame. But as you work through the season of spring in your relationship, it is important to have healthy expectations of what it means
to be attracted to your partner, and how that might feel.

Attraction Is Much More Than Physical

When it comes to beauty and attraction, you may have heard that
there is a specific ratio of facial proportions that some like to call the
golden ratio. These specific measurements are recognized by our brain,
sending messages of attraction to our amygdala medulla oblongata—
our emotional response center—causing us to see certain things and
people as "beautiful."

While it is interesting to understand the brain chemistry behind
physical attraction, it is important for us to keep this concept in proper
perspective. Every day our definition of beauty is constantly being
influenced, defined, and redefined by the messages that we are receiving all around us. From our entertainment to our peer group, from our
family of origin to our spiritual beliefs, we tend to learn much from the
culture around us about what it means to see someone as beautiful or
physically attractive.[1]

True attraction, on the other hand, is multifaceted. It's never based
on physical attraction alone, although physical attraction is a part of
the equation. It has a component of growth in that as two people

interact, share, and connect with one another, attraction is something that will always bloom and grow when the relationship is moving in the right direction.

The Laws of Attraction

The season of spring is defined by a steady and growing attraction to a specific person. There are so many layers and levels to attraction, and the whole is always greater than the sum of its parts. Let's take a look at the different dimensions that I call the laws of attraction because each one of them is an important component in the equation of genuine attraction.

Law 1: Physical Attraction

Real beauty runs deep and is more than external aesthetics. But physical attraction is an important ingredient in the season of spring. Typically, physical attraction is the first thing that draws you to someone because it's the law of attraction that's most obvious to observe.

Back when I was single, I would often imagine what my future relationship was going to be like. I wondered about the kind of guy I'd end up dating and marrying. I'd try to picture who he would be and how he would look. I wondered if when I eventually had a picture of him, would I be proud to show it to my friends, or would I find myself with someone with an amazing heart whom I struggled to find attractive? I know I'm not alone in that worry because I hear from many people who express the same fears and concerns. But finding someone to whom you are physically attracted is an important part of the equation of a healthy relationship. I am thankful that I am married to a man that I find attractive. But I was surprised by my deep attraction to him because he was not my so-called "type." I thought my type was blond-haired and blue-eyed. John was tall and dark. I'm so thankful I was able to see beyond the "type" I would normally find attractive and open my heart to someone who was outside my preferred traits.

Physical attraction is a legitimate need in a relationship, but it must be kept in proper perspective. We're made to believe that physical attraction is supposed to feel magical. We envision two people who are completely enthralled with one another and can't keep their hands off of each other. We imagine sexual ecstasy, infatuation, and that "head-over-heels" feeling that makes our stomach sink, our knees shake, and our heart throb. But physical attraction means simply one thing: *being drawn toward someone*. Sometimes that physical attraction comes with sparks like fireworks, but other times, it's a steady flame that takes time to build and grow.

With that in mind, it is important to remember that expectations of physical perfection or the fulfillment of selfish fantasy are not realistic. Real people have real bodies, and our expectations must be real as well. As you are looking at your relationship, it is important to make sure that physical attraction is part of the equation, but more importantly, that you are coming to the table with appropriate expectations. This is not about finding a supermodel wife or waiting to marry Mr. Universe.

Recently, I was having a conversation with a single guy in his late thirties who has never been married. We were talking about some of the qualities he was looking for in a woman. He had a pretty decent list of good qualities and Christian character.

"Well, I want a woman who loves the Lord. I want someone who has character and has committed her life to serving Him. I'm really interested in missions, and I want someone with that kind of a selfless heart. Oh, and she *has* to look like a supermodel."

"She has to look like a supermodel?" I repeated in a questioning tone.

"Yeah, looks are important," he replied.

"So basically, you want Mother Theresa in supermodel form?" I summarized.

He chuckled at that comment. But really—isn't that sort of what he was saying?

It's important for us to get real with our expectations. We live in a culture in which the concepts of sexual chemistry and physical attraction have become totally, completely, and irreversibly skewed. The entertainment industry and the pornography culture have completely ravaged our understanding of beauty, and namely, the beauty of a real woman. In a sad way, I expect this of our culture, but this messed-up mentality is starting to seep into the church in a truly concerning way.

Our concept of beauty and sex appeal has been completely distorted over the years to the point where our expectations are just unrealistic. We won't even consider seeing someone through the eyes of physical attraction if they don't measure up to the standard that Hollywood has laid out for us, or to the filters that Instagram has convinced us are real life. But we've got to open our eyes to the fact that the standard we've been fed is so far from reality.

Beauty is fluid. And our desires, as well as the people we will find attractive, are morphed and changed based on the things we allow ourselves to be exposed to. In that regard, we actually have some sort of control over the things we define as attractive and beautiful.

Think about this for a moment: During the Renaissance era, a "beautiful woman" wore a size 16, had extremely pale skin, not a drop of makeup, and displayed some serious curves.[2] These days? Well, I don't have to tell you how much our standards have changed. Our idea of beauty continues to change over the years, based on the things we allow ourselves to be exposed to and the standards society sets for us.

In a culture that is infiltrated with pornography, airbrushed billboards and magazines, plastic surgery, and Instagram filters, our standard of "beauty" has moved so far from the truth that it is causing some major damage to our relational expectations—for both men and women. The more unrealistic images we take in, the more skewed our concept of beauty will be. Single or married, you can expose yourself to so much "fantasy" that real women and real men begin to lose their luster.

The only way to get our expectations moving back to reality is to realize that we need a reset. The reason we say "no" to distorted expectations of attraction is that skin-deep beauty can only last so long. Fast-forward 50, 30, or even 10 years, and your body as well as that of your spouse will have changed, sagged, and likely stretched out beyond recognition. After a few babies, a surgery or two along the way, and the unrelenting process of aging, I can guarantee you one thing: Neither of you will look the same. That is why it is so important to make sure your expectations of physical attraction are kept in check because it is only one part of the equation of lasting attraction.

In marriage, you will see your spouse at their absolute worst. You'll see them in their most natural state—before the hair, before the makeup, before the accessories. You'll see them through the lens of real life, which does not hide morning breath, cellulite, or other imperfections. You will be with your spouse through the days of sickness and exhaustion. What will ultimately define your marriage—and ultimately, your very life—is not the "supermodel status" of your husband or wife, but rather, their character.

> What will ultimately define your marriage—
> and ultimately, your very life—is not
> the "supermodel status" of your husband
> or wife, but rather, their character.

Your spouse is the person who will have the greatest influence on your happiness, your confidence, and your security. Your spouse is the person who will walk with you through the highs and lows of life, help raise your children, and influence your family in every single way. According to Proverbs, a wife (or husband) of character is a treasure (Proverbs 31:10). And he who finds that finds a great thing, something worth holding onto no matter what. I know so many marriages that started with "amazing physical chemistry" and fizzled into nothing within a few short years. I also know of so many marriages that started on the foundation of good character and godliness—and continued to grow in intimacy, in respect, and in love.

It is time for us to rise above the noise of this culture and set our relationship expectations and standards on things that really matter. It is time to reset our standard of beauty by shutting off the influence of the unrealistic junk and filling our minds and hearts with the truth.

- Beauty is fleeting (Proverbs 31:30).
- Charm is deceptive (Proverbs 31:30).
- Real beauty runs deep (1 Peter 3:3).

- Real attraction is multifaceted.
- Inner beauty *cannot* be fabricated or replicated.
- Character is what actually defines a person.
- Spiritual health trumps everything (1 Timothy 4:8).

It is time for us to say "no" to the unrealistic standards this world is throwing our way. That starts with taking inventory of what we allow our minds to think about and our hearts to lust upon. Maybe that means making the commitment to stay away from porn. Maybe that means turning off Netflix for a while. Maybe it means stepping away from Facebook or TV or magazines. Maybe that means putting limits on how much we mindlessly scroll Instagram. Maybe it means guarding our conversations and how we allow ourselves to talk about the opposite sex.

Ultimately, it means saying no to lies that skew our perception of physical attraction—in exchange for truth. It's time to reset our understanding of the role of physical attraction in our romantic relationships.

Law 2: Personal Attraction

Have you ever met someone who seemed very attractive until you started interacting with them? A huge part of being drawn to another person comes down to what I call the law of personal attraction. A person's "persona" or "personality" is like a window into their soul. The way they act, interact, behave, communicate, speak, joke, think, express, socialize, and process are the things that make a person who they are. Finding someone with a complementary personality is an important part of a healthy romantic relationship.

When I was growing up, holidays were always a big to-do in my family. They were a special time to gather with grandparents, cousins, uncles, and aunts (and a few random people who always made their way onto the invitation list). One of the things I loved most about these big family gatherings was getting to see all different types of personalities in action.

At any given gathering, there was always that "life-of-the-party" uncle, cracking jokes and making people laugh at every chance. And then there was the "heart-to-heart" cousin, who would much rather get you cornered, ask you a million questions, and somehow bring to the surface your deepest, darkest secrets. There were always the extroverts in the crowd, making their rounds and making small talk with every person they possibly could. And then there were the introverts in the family, desperately trying to find a pocket of peace and quiet among the chaos just so they could get a moment to breathe.

As fascinating as it can be observing the scope of personality types at gatherings like this, it is just as important to understand where you fit on the personality spectrum. Understanding your personality is a huge piece to the puzzle of recognizing the personality types with which you are most (and least) compatible. As much fun as it might be hanging around that guy who is constantly the life of the party, cracking joke after joke and absorbing the spotlight, being married to someone like that may not be a good fit for your personality. As cathartic as conversing for hours on end with heart-to-heart Suzy might be, being married to someone like her may come with its own set of struggles when you try to push the pause button on the deep conversations and realize it doesn't exist. Personalities come in all different shapes, colors, and sizes, and knowing who you are is the key to understanding the type of person who fits into your life.

Our personality is the lens through which we see the world. Carl Jung argued that human beings tend to perceive the world through different psychological types.[3] These basic types of personality were integrated into an assessment that is commonly known today as the Myers-Briggs Type Indicator (MBTI). The MBTI is used by counseling professionals across the country as a tool to help people understand and differentiate their key personality components. According to the MBTI, there are four key components[4] to a person's personality:

Introverted (I) or Extroverted (E)? The terms "introvert" and "extrovert" have become quite common in our vocabulary today, but often these terms have been misinterpreted to refer to whether or not an individual enjoys interacting with people. But introversion and extroversion have nothing to do with our desire for relationships. Both introverts and extroverts are human beings made in God's image, with an innate desire for relationships. The terms "introvert" and "extrovert" refer not to your desire for relationships but to your focus toward the world. Do you tend to focus on the world around you or the world inside of you? Do you look to your relationships and interactions to fill you up and get you energized, or do you look inside yourself, preferring alone time and quiet to recharge and rest? This is a key component in understanding your personality.

Intuitive (N) or Sensing (S)? Another aspect of personality, according to the MBTI is in a person's tendency to process information. Intuitive people are more interested in gathering information based on what they are experiencing and gathering internally. They like to read between the lines and trust their gut and their instinct more than anything else. Sensing people process information by looking at the facts. They're in tune with their physical world more than anything, absorbing and processing everything they hear, see, touch, and experience. They are practical people through and through.

Thinking (T) or Feeling (F)? This aspect of your personality refers to how you make your decisions. Thinkers are commonly head over heart and tend to make choices based on what they know to be true, rather than what they feel. They analyze everything, approach life with logic, and pursue truth at all costs. Feelers make their choices by trusting their heart to lead the way. They value relationships over rules and sentiment over sensibility. They look to their closest relationships, their emotions, and their general longing for peace and harmony as their primary motivation in the decisions they make.

Judging (J) or Perceiving (P)? This last aspect of personality refers to how you structure your life. People who are the judging type are task oriented, scheduled, and structured. They thrive on deadlines, plans, and checklists. They plan out their life and focus on their goals. Perceivers are flexible and spontaneous. They are adaptable and can change plans to accommodate as necessary. They prefer freedom in their work and play rather than being inhibited by deadlines and rigid goals.

The Myers-Briggs Type Indicator takes your preferred psychological type from each of the four categories and puts the letters together to give you a four-letter combination, pointing to one of 16 different personality types. While the 16 types are not the end-all and be-all of your personality, they give you a good gauge of who you are and how you are wired. It is important to understand your personality bent because it informs so much of what you do and how you do it. Personality types can also give you a good idea of what you may need in someone in order to be relationally compatible.

When it comes to attraction in relationships, the old adage that opposites attract often rings true. We tend to be drawn to people who have the qualities, strengths, and personality traits that we lack. To a degree, that natural attraction is healthy and good because in the best of relationships, you find that you are better together. The only problem with opposites attracting is that the same qualities that once attracted you ultimately end up being the qualities that begin to annoy you. Opposites attract, but then they attack.

My husband, John, and I are very similar in a lot of ways, but in other ways, we are total opposites. For instance, I'm structured; he's laid back. I process things out loud; he likes to process internally. I'm more serious; he's more fun. I see the glass half empty; he sees it half full.

Interestingly enough, many of our differences are the things that bless our relationship the most, but they are also the areas that can bring the most tension to our marriage. Everyone tells you that opposites attract, but what they don't tell you is that those very same differences will also attack your relationship if you are not careful.

The more opposites you are dealing with in a relationship, the more you have to learn to see life through the other person's eyes, to hear their heart, to communicate well, to make room for the opinion of another, to consider that maybe your way is not the best way, to sacrifice, to learn, and to grow. Each difference is another opportunity for intimacy, yet also another opportunity for isolation.

As much as I love the concept of personality and identifying personality differences, I'm a firm believer that we live our best life when we are in balance. I love how this little gem from Scripture puts it: "Whoever fears God will avoid all extremes" (Ecclesiastes 7:18). Understanding our personality and tendencies is a first step, but learning to live a life of balance is the ultimate goal—balance in how we act, think, feel, and interact with the world around us. Our personalities may influence us, but they don't define us, and we have the final say in the strengths we choose to absorb and the weaknesses we choose to repel. Finding balance is important for maintaining healthy relationships as well. Maintaining a relationship with someone who is the complete opposite of you in every single aspect of life is just as difficult as when you are entirely the same.

I like to imagine that the healthiest relationships look like a Venn diagram, with just the right balance of differences and similarities between two people.

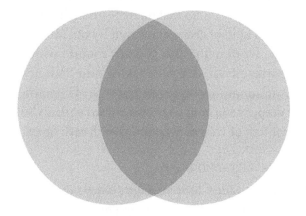

Every good relationship needs enough difference to learn and grow from one another, yet enough similarities to be able to connect with and understand one another. Learning to recognize those similarities and differences in choosing a relationship and then continuing to cultivate them while maintaining a relationship is an important part of the balancing act of personal attraction. As you work through the season of spring, be sure to take a good assessment of the personality that is shining through you, and how it is influencing and impacting those around you.

Law 3: Mental/Emotional Attraction

The season of spring is marked by how two people connect. Mental and emotional attraction is a key component to ongoing attraction in a relationship, keeping love afloat even during times when physical attraction may wane. I recently saw an elderly married couple out in public and noticed very quickly that the silver-haired, elderly husband had his soft, wrinkled hand nonchalantly (yet passionately) grasping the rear end of his silver-haired, elderly wife. The sweet attraction between them seemed so strong despite the wrinkles, the sagging, and the grays. There is a string of attraction holding them together that is far deeper than the physical attraction that once brought them together— the power of mental and emotional connection between two people.

A mental and emotional attraction to another person is defined by your mutual ability to reach beyond the superficial conversations and into the deeper levels of things that matter—thoughts, ideas, opinions, and feelings. This kind of deep connection is both satisfying and stimulating at once. Do you find that you can connect with one another on these important levels? Are you making time and carving out the space in your relationship to cultivate this type of interaction? As your relationship deepens and your commitment strengthens, so should the nature and content of your conversations with each other.

Law 4: Spiritual Attraction

I took a survey asking Christian singles to tell me what they thought was the most important aspect of a dating relationship out of the four laws of attraction. The majority of respondents (46 percent) reported that having a spiritual connection with someone was the most important aspect of attraction when it came to a dating relationship.[5] And I would absolutely agree with that assessment.

When it comes to spiritual attraction in dating, I'm simply referring to the "spiritual overflow" of a person's life. When a person is in love with Jesus, their faith, beliefs, and character ultimately shine through everything they do. They live with purpose and a passion that is not limited to their romantic relationship but exudes into all their life. This is the most significant part of attraction because it's an aspect that infiltrates every other part of the relationship. Find a person to whom you are spiritually attracted and with whom you are spiritually in sync because for a significant relationship to progress to marriage, this must be the component that holds the other aspects of attraction firmly in place. We'll address the topic of spiritual connection in greater detail a little further in the book.

When Attraction Is Missing

But what if the season of spring comes with only a little bit of attraction, or maybe no attraction at all? I got an e-mail from a man who was struggling with the definition of attraction. He had been developing a friendship with an incredible woman; in fact, he described her as "the best woman" he'd ever met. She was smart, pretty, and godly. Not only that, but his friends were also telling him that she was totally right for him. But he just didn't feel that spark of attraction. So, what do you make of your relationship when you don't "got that loving feeling"?

When attraction is missing in a relationship, it is important to take it as a sign that something in the relationship is not as it should be. If you find yourself struggling with a lack of feelings of attraction to your partner, here are some important questions to consider.

Do I have appropriate expectations?

As we examine our expectations, we should take inventory of the things that have shaped our views. If we've been influenced by steamy rom-coms and raunchy reality shows (causing unrealistic emotional expectations), superspiritual literature and legalistic dogma (causing unrealistic spiritual expectations), or pornography and the oversexualization of media (causing unrealistic physical expectations), it is important to make sure that our desires are rooted in reality, not fantasy.

It is important to keep your standards high while learning to differentiate between things that are "majors" (things you should never settle for) and "minors" (things with which you can be lenient) in your relationship.[6] Unrealistic expectations will never translate into fulfilling relationships.

Is there an underlying issue in this relationship?

My friend Rachel struggled off and on with feelings of attraction toward the guy she was dating. She would always vent about it, feeling tons of guilt because she could not pinpoint why she did not feel the longing and attraction she wanted to have in this relationship.

After almost 18 months of internal struggle, she finally decided to take a step back and call off the relationship. Looking back on her relationship, she realized that there was never a strong spiritual attraction between her and this man. She could never connect with him the way she wanted to and did not ever feel like they were on the same page with their faith. One of the laws of attraction was missing, and it made all the difference.

When it comes to the season of spring, sometimes a lack of attraction signifies an underlying issue or a deficit in the relationship. Spring is the best time to come to terms with this reality and, in a dating relationship, make the decision to move on.

Is there an underlying issue within me?

But what if a lack of enthusiasm in spring is more of the norm than the outlier? What if you find yourself struggling in *every* relationship in which you find yourself, pushing away perfectly fine relationships out of fear, confusion, or doubt?

One of the best lessons I learned about relationships is that the most important person you could ever date is yourself. The concept of "dating inward" is actually one of the main topics in my first book, *True Love Dates*. "Dating inward" is based on the idea that you cannot know what you need in a relationship until you know who you are.

Many people struggle to feel a connection in the season of spring and have a hard time navigating through the other seasons because they have not taken the time to date inward. Sometimes we spend so much time looking out that we forget to look in. But when you don't know who you are or where you are headed, you'll never get a good feel for the kind of person who fits into the story of your life.

This lack of understanding and awareness, paired with our past wounds and mistakes, can set us up for some serious fears of rejection, commitment, abandonment, and even fear of failure as we approach our relationships. If you find yourself stuck in a pattern of fear, doubt, or confusion, consider investing in a time of counseling and of dating inward for healing, for direction, and for a chance to really get to know yourself.[7]

You Attract What You Are

An important concept of attraction is that we have some power in the equation of our relationships. Human beings are magnetic, and we tend to attract and be drawn to people who are similar to us physically, emotionally, and spiritually. Our health in each of those categories determines a lot about the type of things we allow in our relationships as well as the kind of people we let into our lives. The healthier you are in these categories, the healthier your relationships will also be. Conversely, your lack of health in these areas will have a negative impact on the type of relationships you choose and of which you allow yourself to be a part.

> Human beings are magnetic, and we tend to attract and be drawn to people who are similar to us physically, emotionally, and spiritually.

If you find yourself in a dating relationship that is not blooming, take a step back and ask yourself why this relationship is not showing signs of life. The good things that are blooming in your life will likely begin to attract the right kind of people—and repel all the rest. Are you blooming in your spiritual and emotional connection with God and with others? If the health of your relationship reflects your personal health, what steps do you need to take to move toward health and healing in your own life? What is God's role in your life, and how have you been moving in His direction? Taking responsibility for your role in a relationship is a sign of maturity and a reminder that you are 50 percent of the equation of a healthy relationship. You are not responsible for the other party, but you are responsible for yourself. Your one and only job is to get yourself healthy and look for someone who is doing the same. When you are not seeing the right qualities and characteristics blooming in someone's life, it is time to set boundaries and limits and surround yourself with people who are moving in God's direction. "Bad company corrupts good character" (1 Corinthians 15:33), so learning to move away from dead-end relationships and instead investing in life-giving relationships is a discipline that will literally change your life.

But what if you find yourself in a marriage that's not blooming? Maybe you started strong with the attraction that comes in the season of spring, but find that you are slowly losing that connection. You both have good intentions, but life, stress, kids, and schedules have gotten in the way. The process of reconnecting in marriage is not something that happens overnight, but every day is an opportunity to add another string to the list of things holding you together and keeping you close. Just as I said above, it starts with asking hard questions, realizing your role, and recognizing your power in the relationship because helplessness will always lead to hopelessness.

Maybe the problem is something that needs to be addressed in the relationship. In a recent survey I took of 1000 married people, I found that over 70 percent of couples spent less than 60 minutes a week connecting on a meaningful level, with a majority of those reporting closer to 0-30 minutes.[8] The lack of emotional connection is one of the most significant detractors from attraction in marriage and has to be addressed first and foremost because all the other laws of attraction hinge on this connection in marriage.

If you dig deep, you may find that the problem is something that needs to be addressed in your own heart. Maybe you are struggling emotionally, spiritually, or physically. Maybe you've allowed your heart to be distracted by other obligations and relationships—such as your children, or even your ministry. Maybe your spirit is divided between your need to connect with God and the demands of this world—such as your career or your schedule. Maybe you've found your mind to be darkened by unhealthy influences and lustful thoughts—such as pornography or your entertainment choices. There are many components that could be influencing and preventing your relationship from blooming, and it is important to take inventory of the unhealthy behaviors in your life that need to be pruned for the healthy things in your life to begin to bloom. You must realize that no matter what season you are in in your marriage, you control 50 percent of the equation. The healthier you become as an individual, the healthier your relationship will become as well.

> The healthier you become as an individual, the healthier your relationship will become as well.

Spring is a time of blooming. It is a time of investing in the good things and pruning out the rest—making room for attraction at its best.

Reflection Questions for Couples

1. When did we move into the season of spring? How was this stage initiated in our relationship?

2. What have we believed about chemistry and attraction? How has culture influenced our beliefs and expectations?

3. What steps can we take to make more time for our emotional connection throughout the week? Which law of attraction do we need to invest in to work toward "attraction at its best" in our relationship?

4. Is there anything unhealthy in our personal lives or in our relationship that we need to "prune" in order to allow for healthy things to blossom?

Reflection Questions for Singles

1. What have I believed about chemistry and attraction? How has culture influenced my beliefs and expectations?

2. Which law of attraction have I neglected the most in

pursuit of a healthy dating relationship? Which law of attraction have I neglected most in my own personal life?

3. Have I taken the time to "date inward"? Are there any wounds or past baggage that seem to be impacting my relationships with my friends, family, or dating relationships?

4. Is there anything unhealthy in my life that I need to prune in order to make room for healthy relationships?

3

THE PATTERN OF GROWTH IS GIVE-AND-TAKE

'm an expert at killing—plants, that is. No matter what I do, I cannot seem to keep my plants alive. They call it having a black thumb, and I have officially self-diagnosed myself as having one. I'm not sure how I ended up with a black thumb because my mother is a plant expert. Her thumb is greener than all thumbs. She has plants in her house that are probably older than I am.

I love having greenery around my house, so I've continued to try bringing plants home with the hopes that I'll eventually get the hang of keeping them alive. *Plants don't need much*, I tell myself, *just some sunshine, oxygen, and water.* I put my new plants in our sunroom, ensuring they'll get plenty of sun. *Sunshine, check!* Lo and behold, my sunroom also happens to have an abundance of air, *check, check!* So really, all I need to do is water them, right? *This isn't so bad*, I tell myself. *I can do this.*

Yet, what ends up happening every time is that I forget to water them. Life is full of other things I need to do, and somehow, those little plants get neglected and ignored. And then they die. Like I said, I'm an expert at killing plants.

Eventually, my husband, John, came up with a brilliant plan. He did some research and found out that there's a type of plant that doesn't actually need much water. In fact, it will thrive on less. Water it once a week, and it will do just great! It is made to be neglected. It's called a succulent. John bought me three beautiful succulents to put on our kitchen table. Each of the three succulents had a similar cactus look but was unique in its own way, with different-shaped leaves, beautiful hues of green, and textures that ranged from glossy to velveteen. I'm not sure which part we enjoyed more: seeing them brighten up our kitchen table or just having fun saying their names. I'm pretty sure I heard the phrase, "Your succulents are looking nice and plump today" coming from my husband daily, with a wink.

I loved those succulents. And truth be told, I kept them alive for far longer than I expected. But a few weeks into it, my black thumb kicked into full gear. I started forgetting whether or not I had watered them for the week. *Did I water them on Monday? Or was that last Monday? Hmmm. I'm not sure. I can't remember. Oh well, I'll just water them to be on the safe side.* And so I would water them, even though I could not remember if it was the first or the second time that week. Eventually, I found out that there must have been a few too many "second times" because my poor succulents' roots got so moist they rotted. And then, my succulents died. All three of them. If you walk into my kitchen today, you'll find another large, beautiful bowl of succulents. Except when you get close enough, you'll realize that they're plastic succulents. Because apparently, that's about all I can handle. Plants require three things to live: sunlight, oxygen, and water. Too little, and they can't grow. But too much, and they will die.

The Give-and-Take of Growth

Like plants, relationships require a pattern of give-and-take in order for them to grow. If you are in a relationship in which you are constantly taking and never giving anything in return, your relationship will eventually stop growing. On the converse, if you are in a relationship in which you are doing all the giving and getting nothing in return, your relationship will soon die. This type of pattern cannot be maintained in nature or in relationships. Healthy relationships have to be made up of just the right amount of giving and taking. Spring is an important season because it is the time to assess the pattern of give-and-take in your closest relationships.

One-Sided Relationships

Recently on my *Love + Relationships* podcast, I was chatting with a young woman struggling with a pattern of one-sided relationships. She was giving, investing, initiating, and interacting—but getting little to nothing in return. "I seem to be doing all the work in my relationships," she said. I know she's not alone in this because I hear from a lot of people who are dealing with similar relationships. One e-mail I received went something like this: "I've been involved in this relationship for five years, and I'm starting to come to terms with the reality that it isn't much of a relationship at all. I've been committed to him, but he hasn't committed to me."

One-sided relationships consist of two people, but only one person is doing most of the work. It is an unfortunate problem that even more unfortunately occurs far too often.

Maybe it is the man who has been saying he loves you for years but is never willing or ready to commit.

Maybe it is that friend who says she wants to be a part of your life but never asks, never reaches out, and never initiates.

Maybe it is that guy who has been privately texting you for months, but when you see him face-to-face, he acts like you don't exist.

Maybe it is that girlfriend who says she is done with the guys in her past but can't seem to keep those boundaries firm and those doors closed.

Maybe it is the boyfriend who wants to keep taking physically but giving nothing back emotionally.

Maybe it is the spouse who avoids emotional intimacy by investing everything into their ministry or career, neglecting to invest in their closest relationships.

I could list a hundred examples, and I'm sure you could too. But the bottom line about one-sided relationships is that they are relationships in which one person always seems to be doing all the giving—the forgiving and forgetting, the initiating, the investing, the ignoring, the working through—while the other person seems to be doing all the taking.

Giving Too Much

The interesting thing about one-way relationships is that no matter who is doing the giving or taking, it always takes two people to keep them going. Behind every one-sided relationship there is a person who is giving too much and expecting too little. A person who continues to make excuses. A person who continues to see the relationship for what it could be, rather than what it actually is. A person who is failing to set proper expectations and healthy boundaries.

Some of you are reading this and nodding your head in agreement. But I know there are others of you that are not so sure. "Debra, can you really 'give too much' as a Christian? Aren't we called to love like Jesus? Shouldn't we give, and give, and give—expecting nothing in return?" For some of you, the idea of setting limits and boundaries in your life is a hard one to grasp. You see love as an unconditional aspect of relationships, and rightly so. But loving someone does not mean allowing them to have a free pass to do what they want, when they want, how they want it, with little to no consequences. Love does not mean that we enable an unhealthy relationship, allowing someone to take advantage of us, hurt us repeatedly, or use and abuse us in the name of "selflessness."

> Love does not mean that we enable
> an unhealthy relationship.

Far too often, people mistake selflessness with passivity, and it is a costly mistake. But selflessness does not mean ignoring your needs or keeping them to yourself. It doesn't mean staying silent and expecting others to know what you want or need. And it doesn't mean holding back, particularly when speaking up could be beneficial to your personal health and the health of your relationship. Healthy relationships are defined by give-and-take, and being a person who only gives and never takes is living a passive life, not a selfless one. It's up to you to identify your needs and then express them in a respectful, assertive, and loving way.

Not only is a giving-too-much mentality unhealthy for the giver, it is also unhealthy for the taker. It fuels a pattern of dysfunction in a relationship, rather than calling the relationship and the people involved in that relationship to a better place. It enables the taker to continue behaving in a harmful way without challenging them to get healthy. And just like the plant that received too much water, a relationship with a pattern of give-give-give won't be able to sustain itself and will eventually die.

There are many reasons why a person gives too much in a relationship, but I'm going to narrow them down to three types of people that I've seen in my clinical experience.

The Rescuer

Brent was a rescuer. He had a long history of romantic relationships in which he ended up with a shattered heart. All his life, he was known as the boy with the big heart. And now, that "big heart" was broken, and it was starting to have a negative impact on his health and well-being.

Brent loved taking care of people. He saw people for who they could be, rather than who they were. He could look past their troublesome behavior or bad habits and see their potential. If something (or someone) was broken, Brent wanted to fix it. Fixing things and solving problems brought him a lot of fulfillment. Consequently, he tended to go for the girls that "needed fixing" in his dating relationships as well. In a way, Brent was trying to be their savior, failing to realize that there is really only One who can save (Acts 4:12). And that is where his problems began. Time and time again he found himself in relationships that he couldn't fix. Though he would try, and try, and try to win them over with his love, he would ultimately fail because you can't get someone to change when they really don't want to change. Even while he was able to fix little things here and there, he could never ultimately give these women what they really needed: true healing. Relationship after relationship, he found himself the recipient of abuse, abandonment, infidelity, and betrayal.

My heart goes out to people like Brent—people who try so hard to fix the world around them, often at the expense of their own health and well-being. Rescuers usually come from a past in which there was a situation or a person who needed fixing. Maybe it was a parent or family member struggling with alcoholism, mental illness, or physical problems, who couldn't seem to help themselves. Maybe it was witnessing their parents' broken marriage, the experience of seeing the problems but no solutions. Maybe there was a death or loss or grief in their lives, and they wanted so desperately to take away the pain. Whatever it is, rescuers grow up believing that it is their job to fix the world around them. That mentality often spills over into their romantic relationships. Rescuers have a hard time implementing boundaries. They have a hard time saying to their loved ones, "This is your problem to fix. I love you, and I'm here for you, and I'll support you. But you have to fix this yourself." And with that, they end up giving, and giving, and giving.

The Pleaser

Pleasers love to be loved. They love to be loved so much that they'll do almost anything to get that feeling of love and acceptance. They are utterly loyal to the people in their lives, so much so that they are willing to make excuses and fill in the blanks when their closest relationships fall short. Pleasers hate conflict and confrontation. Conflict makes them uncomfortable and causes them to question whether they are loved and accepted. Rather than deal with conflict, they do whatever it takes to avoid conflict, even if that means giving too much and expecting too little. Pleasers are usually very sensitive people, hyperaware of their emotions and the feelings of those around them. They are so desperate not to hurt anyone close to them that they don't take the opportunity to express what they need. They would much rather be the ones who end up hurt than hurting someone they love. Oftentimes, that is exactly what happens. They end up disillusioned, hurt, and empty.

The Insecure

An important part of learning to expect more from our relationships is understanding our value and worth in Jesus because so often we attract the type of relationships we think we deserve. There are a lot of people out there struggling to believe that they deserve better. "This must be as good as it gets," they convince themselves. They have such a low sense of value and self-worth that they don't even comprehend that healthy relationships of give-and-take can exist. Oftentimes, this insecurity is rooted in the experiences of our past. Maybe we walked through relationships in which we were put down, shamed, or made to believe that we weren't good enough. So many times, we begin believing those negative labels that get placed on us and living out those lies rather than exposing them.

For the young woman I mentioned earlier in this chapter who was struggling in one-sided relationships, saying "no" to the lies from her past and understanding her value and worth in Jesus was a huge part of the process of expecting more from her relationships. Because of Jesus at work in her life and the high value He placed on her, she began to realize that she deserved relationships in which she felt reciprocal love, respect, honesty, and initiative. It *wasn't* too much to ask. Grasping that truth begins to transform our perspective on relationships and holds us to a higher standard—the good standard to which we are called. "For we are his workmanship, created in Christ Jesus for good works..." (Ephesians 2:10 ESV). We were made for good works. We were made for good things. We were made for good relationships.

Giving Too Little

Maybe you are reading through some of these descriptions above, and you just can't relate because you usually find yourself on the other side of the spectrum: the taking side, which often means you give too little, distancing yourself from relationships. When it comes to people who give too little in relationships, here are the types of people I tend to see.

The Cynic

There's a commonly used phrase that goes something like this:

There are two reasons why I don't trust people.

1. I don't know them.

2. I know them.

Maybe you can relate to that mentality. It is a mentality that I can fall into myself, if I am not careful. Cynics live by the mantra that people cannot be trusted. They are skeptical of relationships and keep people at a distance for that reason. Afraid of letting people in, they build a wall around themselves as a way to keep safe but find themselves isolated and alone. It is important to display a healthy caution in relationships and give trust only as trust is earned. But cynics are not driven by healthy caution: They are driven by debilitating fear. They may fear getting hurt, they may fear rejection, or they may fear abandonment or betrayal.

Most cynics have real reason to be mistrusting. Somewhere along the road of relationships, they've been abandoned, hurt, or betrayed. The experience could have come from a parent, a close friend, or a significant other—but the experience left them with an inability to fully let their guard down again.

I counseled a young woman who fit this definition of a cynic. She grew up in a family in which the father was a "part-time dad," as she referred to him. Most of the time, he was away with other women, stuck in a cycle of infidelity and sexual affairs. She watched how his behavior tore up her mother's heart and vowed that she would never let that happen to her. Growing up with a father figure like that left her with the message that men couldn't be trusted. If she couldn't trust her own father, whom could she trust? She was being trained to be cynical from the earliest years of her life.

In the years that followed, the Lord did a transforming work in this young woman's heart, and brought her to a place of healing in her own life and relationships. She met a wonderful, God-honoring man, and they moved forward toward marriage. But even so, she found herself struggling with cynicism, unable to trust her husband-to-be, even though he had proven to be loyal, trustworthy, and faithful. She was not able to give fully because she was struggling to trust fully. In order to overcome her tendency to give too little, I had to remind her of the importance of distinguishing the *false* alarms from the *true* alarms. She had become so accustomed to not trusting that even when it was *safe* to trust, her mind continued to sound the alarm. Her journey of healing meant learning to recognize and understand the difference between someone who is trustworthy and someone who is not.

The Wounded

There is truth to the clever adage that "hurt people hurt people." When you are wounded, you tend to wound others also. That is an important lesson for all of us to remember, especially in how we relate to the world around us. Have you ever interacted with someone who was just miserable to be around? I remember one time I was picking up food from a restaurant and noticed that my server was just huffing and puffing through the entire interaction. Every time I ordered something or asked for something else, her facial expressions, eye-rolling, slamming of my food items, and sighing noises communicated that I was just the absolute biggest inconvenience in her day. She was short, unkind, and downright rude. My first reaction to this woman was to think, *Wait until she sees the size of her tip with that attitude. That will really annoy her.* But then the Holy Spirit convicted my heart. I had no idea what she had been through that day. I'm not excusing rude behavior, but let's acknowledge that maybe there's more to the story than our eyes can see. Maybe she got a call with news of terrible test results from her doctor. Maybe she just lost a loved one. Maybe she was struggling in an abusive relationship or marriage. I had no clue what her story was that day, and my job was simply to repay evil with blessing (1 Peter 3:9).

Wounded people tend to wound other people. Sometimes people who give too little do so because they are struggling with a gaping wound in their heart that they haven't dealt with or even recognized. In order to be people that engage in healthy give-and-take relationships, we need to recognize our wounds and move toward healing and wholeness because hurt people hurt people, but *healed* people bring healing to the lives and relationships around them.

The Empty

Have you ever felt so tired, exhausted, drained, or empty that you had nothing left to give? Have you ever felt as though every drop of energy and motivation had been squeezed out of your life? I know I've felt that way before, particularly after I became a mom. Being a parent is hard enough, and having our kids 20 months apart took it to a whole new level. Those early years of parenting are somewhat of a blur: the sleepless nights, the never-ending diapers, the round-the-clock feedings. All day, every day, the demands of caring for two little ones required an amount of selflessness I didn't even know I possessed. It took every drop out of me, and I often found myself living on empty in those early years.

There were times when my husband, John, would come home after a long day of work, and I felt like I had given everything to the kids all day and that I had absolutely nothing left to give when he walked in the door. *There's nothing left, hon. They've taken it all.* I was too tired to be peppy, too exhausted to be talkative, and too drained to interact. I learned pretty quickly that if I was to keep my marriage healthy and strong, I needed to make getting recharged a priority. I learned to prioritize my time with Jesus (the ultimate Giver of life and fullness), to invest in things that I loved (writing and ministry), and to surround myself with friends, family, and moms' groups (support, support, support!). I couldn't live on empty and expect my marriage to stay in a good place. I had to make sure I was filled because empty people make terrible partners.

> I couldn't live on empty and expect my marriage to stay in a good place. I had to make sure I was filled because empty people make terrible partners.

We can engage in one-way relationships when we fail to recognize our need to be filled. When one person in the relationship is giving themselves to the point of feeling empty yet never taking the time or effort to get refilled, eventually the relationship will lose its reciprocity. Maybe they're giving themselves to their job, their ministry, or their hobbies. Maybe their schedules are out of control, they're feeling pulled in every direction, and they are finding themselves spread way too thin. Whatever it is, the bottom line is that empty people give too little because they don't feel like they have enough to give.

Pursuing healthy relationships means recognizing our emptiness and making it a priority to get filled. We should take time to rest, to reenergize, and to take care of ourselves without feeling guilty about it. Pursuing healthy relationships means setting boundaries, clearing the schedule, and learning to say "no" to the okay things so we can say "yes" to the best things. We must understand our limitations and be deliberate about sitting under the Living Water of Jesus through things like the intimate act of prayer, the memorization of Scripture, the power of fasting, the accountability of discipleship, and the discipline of being still. Jesus is truly the only One who can fill us up to overflowing so that we'll never thirst again. In fact, Jesus says that His water will not only fill us, but it will sustain us for eternity: "Whoever drinks the water I give them will never thirst. Indeed, the water I give them will become in them a spring of water welling up to eternal life" (John 4:14).

It is important to take inventory of your level of emptiness periodically and ask yourself how it might be impacting your closest relationships. What do you need to do to get filled? How can you take those next steps?

Pruning the Excess—Learning to Let Go

We're in the middle of a big purge right now. Just this morning, we gave away a full-sized freezer, some wooden bar stools, a brown leather couch, and a bunch of house decorations. We're getting ready to do some renovations in our basement, and that process has required us to get rid of some unnecessary things so that we can make room for something new.

I'm a person that likes to hold on. I see the memories, experiences, and emotions tied up in the items I have. *Those were the very first shoes our daughter Ella wore to church! That was the shirt I wore to our engagement party! That was our boy's favorite car to play with!* I hold on to memories through the items in my home. (John would call me a shameless hoarder, but I refuse to accept that title. I don't "hoard," I "hold." There's a big difference. Okay, maybe I'm a hoarder in denial. But let's not get caught up on semantics.) Yet oftentimes, it is in the *letting go* that we get to open our hands and hearts to receive something new, a shift of perspective, or growth, healing, and blessings. A sweet friend of mine recently reminded me that "sometimes, a season of purging our physical things is symbolic of the spiritual things God is doing in our life." Those words are ringing through my ears this morning as I ask God what He's doing in my life and in my relationships.

Jesus gives us the perfect imagery of pruning and purging when He said, "I am the true vine, and my Father is the gardener. He cuts off every branch in me that bears no fruit, while every branch that does bear fruit he prunes so that it will be even more fruitful" (John 15:1-2). I live in a farming town, where pruning is a fact of life. There are apple orchards, cherry orchards, and peach orchards on every corner. At the end of every season, any farmer will tell you that if you want your tree to produce good fruit year after year, you have to continually prune it. You have to cut off certain branches that aren't doing well and trim down others in order for them to grow even bigger and better the next season. If you don't, the branches will crowd each other out, and eventually, the entire tree will stop producing good fruit. So much of the Christian life is about pruning the things that are holding us back, cutting off the things that aren't producing fruit, and pruning the good things so that we can do even better things.

Lately, I've found myself praying, *Lord, what else do I need to prune from my life? What are the "good things" that I'm involved in that might be taking the place of the "best things" You have for me? What do I need to prune out of my schedule, my priorities, and my daily routine in order to make more time for the things and the people that matter most? Are there any relationships in my life that are holding me back and keeping me stagnant? Are there people in my life that are distracting me and preventing me from focusing on Your kingdom?*

We need to make it our aim to focus on the growth and prune all the rest.

The Pruning of Relationships

Whether or not you recognize it, there are probably relationships in your life right now that are holding you back. They're holding you back from bearing the good fruit that God intended for you to create. Maybe you are dating someone who isn't engaging in the give-and-take of a healthy relationship on a spiritual or emotional level. They're holding you back, and you know you need to let them go, but you are struggling to do that. Maybe you are navigating a friendship right now with someone who is all about the taking and never the giving. You find yourself drained and empty in the process of doing all the work and getting little to nothing in return. Or, maybe you are in a marriage and you feel like you've tried everything, but the person to whom you are married is unresponsive or unwilling. You're discouraged and ready to give up hope. Where do you go from here? How do you recognize what needs to go and what needs to be tended to?

Though there are no cookie-cutter answers, here are some guidelines to think through as you are praying over the pruning process in your own life and relationships.

Dating

What you see in dating, you will always see in marriage multiplied by a hundred. Contrary to popular belief, dating is actually the "troubleshooting period" by which you are getting to know someone. The problem is, too many people take dating far more seriously than they should, and instead of seeing it as a trial period, they see it as the no-turning-back road to marriage. Once they start down that road, they have a really hard time letting go when the relationship doesn't pan out to be a good fit. We have to learn to see dating as a *part* of the process of finding a healthy relationship. Dating is not the time to establish a lifelong commitment; it is the time to be on the lookout for healthy (or unhealthy) traits in our pursuit of finding a good match for our lives.

Within that process, it is of ultimate importance to date with no regrets by setting emotional, physical, and spiritual boundaries for your dating life so that you are ready and prepared to let go of this relationship the moment you start seeing things that aren't healthy or God-honoring. Dating is not the time to try and salvage a broken relationship; it is the time to build a healthy relationship. If you are not seeing that in the person you are interested in or dating, you likely never will. It is time to let go and move on without guilt.

> Dating is not the time to establish a lifelong commitment; it is the time to be on the lookout for healthy (or unhealthy) traits in our pursuit of finding a good match for our lives.

Friendship

Long before you enter a dating relationship, your friendships pave the way for the type of person you are becoming as well as the type of interactions you will expect in a romantic relationship. Friendships can be used to shape our character and influence our lives, and it's important to go into them expecting a pattern of give-and-take. God calls us to different types of friendship relationships in our life. I like to categorize relationships in three different ways. We have *mentor relationships* with people who are pouring into us and encouraging us. We have *discipleship relationships* with people to whom we're called to minister, pour into, and invest in. And we have *peer relationships* with people who are walking beside us, investing in us, and receiving from us in the give-and-take of healthy relationships. Where we get burnt out is when all our relationships begin resembling *discipleship relationships*. If the majority of your closest relationships are discipleship relationships— ones in which you are giving and giving without receiving—you need to take a second look and ask yourself why. In order for us to maintain healthy relationships and have the energy we need to invest in the people God has called us to, we have to have a close inner circle of peer relationships with people who are engaging in the give-and-take of healthy relationships. If all our relationships are discipleship relationships, we'll find ourselves burnt out and empty.

If you are feeling that emptiness right now, I challenge you to take a hard look at your closest friendships and ask yourself how you can fill those spots with people who are investing in you as much as you are investing in them. Honing this skill in friendship is the best way to learn to apply it to your romantic relationships as well. What kind of boundaries do you need to set in relationships that are draining you? Maybe you need to limit your time with certain people or learn to say "no" to overwhelming commitments in order to prioritize your emotional and spiritual health. Maybe there are certain people in your life who are toxic, and you need to slowly begin to let go. I can't answer those questions for you, but I want to challenge you to think through them for yourself and ask yourself, "Is there anyone in my life who is holding me back and pulling me into a toxic or unhealthy relationship—and what steps do I need to take to begin to let go?"

Marriage

The commitment to become "one flesh" is a lifelong covenant in which we're promising to choose love, to *choose marriage,* no matter what this life may bring. But maybe you find yourself in a marriage that is so far from give-and-take. You're feeling stuck, discouraged, and depleted. The pruning of marriage means taking a good, hard look at what's not working and commit to pruning out the unhealthy branches of things like selfishness, passivity, pride, addictions, isolation, and any other sins or unhealthy behaviors that are holding you back as a couple. In most cases, these "unhealthy branches" can only be recognized and worked through with the help of a professional counselor.

In every marital relationship, there are two flawed people in need of healing—two sinners who are going to bring mistakes, disappointments, and failures into the relationship. While one person may be causing more harm and damage to the relationship than the other, both parties have a responsibility to get themselves to a healthier place as individuals in order for the marriage to move toward a healthy place as a couple. Wherever you are at in your marriage right now, you are only responsible for you—and getting yourself healthy is a big responsibility. When you get healthy, it will ultimately impact your marriage. In order to recognize what changes are needed in your life, you need the help of a third party who can call you out where you are wrong, affirm you where you are right, and give you the support you need. Even if your spouse is not willing to join you in counseling, don't let that be your excuse. You are responsible for your personal health and wholeness, and pruning out the unhealthy branches in your marriage starts with recognizing them in your own life first. Take that next step. Get yourself support. Start the process of moving toward healing again and again and again.

Spring Is Only the Beginning

It is no coincidence that the season of spring is the first season because spring is only the beginning. Spring is the season of planting good seeds, removing harmful weeds, and pruning out the unhealthy things that are crowding out our relationships. It is a season of being in tune to God's Spirit, aligning our heart and our relationships with God and what He is doing. I firmly believe that if we go into the season of spring seeing it as a great investment, we'll come out the other side with a great harvest. We serve a God who can do immeasurably more than all we ask or imagine (Ephesians 3:20), a God who reminds us that no matter what our past, the season of sowing healthy seeds can start in our lives right now, today. For those who "sow righteousness…[will] reap the fruit of unfailing love" (Hosea 10:12). We can be confident of that as we walk forward with great expectations of what God will do one season at a time. Because spring, my friends, is only the beginning.

Reflection Questions for Couples

---

1. In looking at your marriage or relationship, do you tend to give "too much" in a relationship or "too little"?

2. With which of the following types do you identify the most? In what ways do you identify with that description?

    a. The Rescuer

    b. The Pleaser

    c. The Insecure

    d. The Cynic

    e. The Wounded

    f. The Empty

3. Is there any excess you need to prune from your life or schedule to make room for investing in your relationship? Is there anything you need to prune from your life to become healthy? Make a list and then pray, asking God to help you with the process of letting them go.

Reflection Questions for Singles

1. In looking at your closest friendships and relationships, do you tend to give "too much" in a relationship or "too little"?

2. With which of the types listed above do you identify the most? In what ways do you identify with that description?

3. Are there any unhealthy people or unhealthy relationships you need to "prune" from your life to make way for healthy relationships?

Section 2

SUMMER—
THINGS GET HOT

Summer is the season when things get hot: emotionally, sexually, and spiritually. In summer, we start removing our layers little by little, revealing who we really are and what we're all about.

It's the season of intimacy as we learn what it takes to fuel the warmth of emotional connection, to navigate the heat waves of sexual tension, and to fan the fire of spiritual connection. It's a season of intense feelings and strong emotions.

But if we're not careful, the heat of summer also leaves us vulnerable to get burned. From experiencing spiritual and emotional disconnect, to dealing with compatibility issues, to taking sex outside of its intended context—the heat of summer is not something to be played with. You've got to learn how to be protected and prepared in order to navigate this season well.

Summer is a season where things get hot, and its fires can make or break your relationship.

4

WARMTH—THE BOND OF EMOTIONAL CONNECTION

My son is *terrified* of spiders. And at the start of every summer, when those eight-legged little creatures start to come out in all their glory, so does his fear. He's had this phobia ever since he was a toddler. Something about spiders gets him worked up to the point of hysteria. As his counselor-mommy, I've tried to pinpoint exactly where or how this fear started. But I'm at a loss. He's never been bitten by a spider, or even touched one for that matter. He's never had a creepy-crawly-hairy thing inching up his leg or down his back. His phobia is so strong that if he sees a spider's web, even with no spider in it, he'll start to get worked up. Just the sight (or feel) of those little silky strands, and he'll start screaming, running in the other direction.

Lately, we've been helping him try to work through this fear with something that counselors call "exposure therapy." The main idea of exposure therapy is to slowly expose a person to their fear in safe and secure environments. For us, that has meant that we have walked through pet shops, encouraging him to take a peek at the tarantula behind the thick glass tank. We've looked through insect books, paging through the different sections, getting a look at different types of spiders and arachnids from a safe distance. We've even been admiring spider webs lately, pointing out the different strings and strands of silky web, woven together in the most meticulous, deliberate, and awe-inspiring way.

I have to admit that my appreciation of spider webs has grown tremendously in this process of getting an up-close-and-personal look at so many of them. And I've learned a lot about spider webs along the way. Did you know that spiders' web strands are one of the strongest materials on earth? In fact, they are ten times tougher than Kevlar, the material used to make bulletproof vests![1] A spider's silk is literally stronger than steel, to the point that scientists are currently trying to figure out a way to produce artificial spider silk that can be used in hospitals around the world.[2] That's some unbelievably powerful web—thousands of little strands, woven together, stronger than steel.

The Bond of Summer

Something about that imagery really resonates with me when I think about the season of summer because it is the season where the web of a relationship begins to develop. I like to picture my relationship with my husband as a collection of thousands of invisible strings holding us together. The strands began in the very early stages of our friendship, increased through our dating, and continue to be formed and developed throughout our marriage. Like that little spider, every day we choose to add additional strands to the structure we are building together, the strong web that holds us together. Summer is a time to begin constructing those strings, relying upon the foundation that was laid in spring. It is the time in a relationship where things begin to heat up as the strings of connection begin to develop between two people one strand at a time, starting with their emotional connection.

Emotional connection is something we don't talk about often in relationships, though it is one of the most important aspects of maintaining a healthy relationship through every age and stage. When it comes to romantic relationships, in the Christian context we are far more likely to talk about physical connection or spiritual connection— but emotional connection somehow gets lost in the conversation.

In every relationship, the strings of emotional connection really start to multiply in the season of summer. You find yourself getting more and more comfortable with the person before you. You feel less inhibited in your communication, more deliberate in your emotional expression, and open to widely expanding your topics of conversation. Summer is when emotions begin to warm up, and each person starts to let down their guard as they get to know each other intimately and deeply. It's a time to be vulnerable and reveal who you really are and what you are all about. In spring, it can be easy to coast and try to be what you think the other person wants you to be. But in the heat of summer, there's really no place to hide. In order to establish emotional connection, you have to start to shed your layers and expose your true self.

Shedding the Layers

I used to really like sports. In fact, just the other day as I was rummaging through my old things for the big "purge" I was telling you about earlier, I found a couple of old sports jerseys I used to wear. Today, I am so far removed from the world of sports that when I found these objects of clothing, I caught myself wondering, *In what world did I like sports enough to own a jersey?*

My six-year-old son made good use of my old jerseys. He instantly put them on (on top of each other) and pranced around the house with joy that he had Mommy's old jerseys. But the clear contrast in my reaction to these items made me realize that sports are clearly no longer an interest in my life. Now that I'm older and wiser, I question if they ever actually were. Deep down, I don't think I liked sports as much as I let on. I am a huge fan of books, I seriously enjoy coffee, I find writing therapeutic, and I have a genuine appreciation of food. But sports? Not so much. Sometimes, I wonder if I was just interested in sports because it's what I thought I was supposed to do, or because it's what the people around me enjoyed, or because it was a way to connect with others.

Have you ever found yourself interested in something just because everyone else around you was interested in it? Or have you ever taken part in something just because the people closest to you were all doing *those things* or acting *that way* or going to *those places*? We allow others to tell us who we should be and what we should like, rather than looking at the reflection in our own mirror. It's almost as though your real self (who you are) gets all tangled up with your perceived self (who you think you should be), and somewhere along the way you start forgetting which side of you is the true side of you. You get lost in the middle. This happens with our romantic relationships more than others. Sometimes, we get so caught up trying to find "the one" that we lose ourselves in the process. We align our likes and dislikes, our hobbies and interests, our personalities and beliefs with that of our potential partner—without taking the time to discover who we are standing alone.

> Sometimes, we get so caught up trying to find "the one" that we lose ourselves in the process.

That's why I love the season of summer in a relationship. Summer is an invitation to shed your emotional layers, come to terms with who you really are, and communicate that authentic side of you to the person with whom you are in a relationship. Not your perceived, preferred, or ideal self—but your real, true self. This isn't an easy process. In fact, some people have such a hard time getting through this vulnerable season that they just skip over it. I worked with a woman who, ten years into marriage, finally realized that she had never taken the time to discover her identity and share her true self with her husband. She had spent so much of her life being what she thought he wanted her to be that she never took the time to find out who she really was. Now, in her late thirties, she found herself struggling through a midlife identity crisis that was wreaking havoc on her personal life, leaving her feeling completely disconnected from her husband. The season of summer invites us to take down the facade and truly connect.

Emotional Connection

Emotional connection is the powerful and crucial force that holds two people together in a relationship. While you may find yourself naturally drawn to someone on an emotional level, it takes effort and opportunity to keep that emotional connection strong. Dr. John Gottman has done extensive research on this subject. For over 40 years, he's been studying the ingredients that make for a healthy relationship. One of the main ideas in all his research is that it is not the grand, romantic gestures that make the best relationships, but the tiny moments of emotional connection throughout the day. Dr. Gottman calls these little things "emotional bids."[3] Emotional bids are the gestures we make and the interactions we have with our spouse in an attempt to connect. They can come in the form of a simple question, such as, "How was your day?" or "What are you reading?" Or, they can come in the form of a statement that is meant to trigger conversation like, "I had a really interesting interaction today." The main idea is that in these bids, we are turning toward our loved one, making the effort to connect. Emotional bids can be accepted (you receive the interaction, respond, and interact back), or rejected (you ignore the interaction, stay quiet, or change the subject). Not surprisingly, in Dr. Gottman's research, the couples who had a higher percentage of accepting and responding to bids were the ones who had the most success in their relationships.[4] That's the power of emotional connection.

> It is not the grand, romantic gestures that make the best relationships, but the tiny moments of emotional connection throughout the day.

But emotional connection takes effort—effort to give and effort to receive. That is something that a lot of couples take for granted. We assume that these things are going to happen naturally, but they don't. Just like that little spider has to put effort, time, and energy into building its web, so also, we must take the time, effort, and energy to invest in our emotional connection. Every interaction you have will either add to your emotional connection or take away from it. When it comes to your most significant relationships, it is up to you to recognize the attitudes, actions, and opportunities that build your connection and make them a regular part of your everyday life. There are so many ways the strings of emotional connection can deepen between two people, but let me share two important ways to connect.

> Every interaction you have will either add to your emotional connection or take away from it. When it comes to your most significant relationships, it is up to you to recognize the attitudes, actions, and opportunities that build your connection and make them a regular part of your everyday life.

Sharing Your Heart

We refer to the word "heart" a lot in Christian lingo. If you think for a moment, I bet you could call to mind at least five phrases that use the word "heart" in some way, shape, or form. *Guard your heart. Protect your heart. Share your heart.* While those may be phrases we hear a lot, the average person doesn't actually know what it means to do those things. What is our heart, anyway? For a term that is so ingrained in our Christian vocabulary, it's a word we often fail to assign meaning. We're clearly not talking about anatomy—the organ that pumps blood to our body—so, what are we talking about?

Studies of this word in Scripture point to the idea that the heart is "the central, defining element of a human person."[5] It is essentially all the different components that make up a person, including their emotions, thoughts, actions, interactions, and behaviors. It is not only who they are, but the way they live their life. The heart is a comprehensive thing, and to know a person is to know their heart. Proverbs 27:19 says, "As water reflects the face, so one's life reflects the heart." In order to begin sharing your heart with someone, you have to begin with the awareness of who you are and what you are all about. Conversation and communication usually start in the shallow end and move deeper as a relationship grows.

There are four distinct levels of communication. Each level offers a little more of who you are and takes you a little deeper in your relationship.

> Level 1: Facts—sharing basic information about you and the world around you.
>
> Level 2: Opinions/Ideas—this level is a little more intimate because it expresses your personal views and offers more of yourself.
>
> Level 3: Feelings—emotions require a deeper level of relationship because expressing feelings is a vulnerable exchange.
>
> Level 4: Faith—sharing about your spiritual beliefs and your relationship with God connects two people in a powerful way.[6]

Each level of conversation takes you deeper, but each level also requires practice because significant and meaningful communication doesn't come naturally for everyone.

I find that the people who struggle most with communication—expressing their heart—are usually the people who have struggled the most with understanding who they are. In order to express your thoughts, you have to know *what* you are thinking. And in order to express your feelings, you have to know *how* you are feeling.

For people who struggle with this concept, I encourage them to start journaling. Each day, take a page of your journal to write about a few topics as you start bringing what's inside to the outside.

Your Thoughts: What are you thinking about lately? What do you find your brain going to when you have nothing to do? Are there topics or subjects on which you have deep opinions and ideas? Write down your thoughts and begin to make some observations. Are your thoughts uplifting or discouraging? Do your thoughts tend to revolve around the negative aspects of a situation or experience or the positive aspects?

Your Feelings: What type of feelings tend to be a part of your daily experience? What things do you feel most strongly about? Writing about your feelings helps you become in tune with them and aware of them. Are you filled most often with sadness or anxiety? Joy and happiness? Discouragement and doubt? What type of things influence your feelings? What are you feeling stressed about? What do you feel excited about?

Your Behaviors: What activities and behaviors are you engaging in with your limited time? Take some time to think through those and write about them. What projects, goals, and dreams are you tackling in your life right now? What steps are you taking in your life, and are those behaviors leading you where you want to go? Are there any behaviors that are problematic or meaningless that you need to get rid of or take out of your life? What are behaviors you could replace them with to take you in the direction where you want your life to go?

Your Interactions: With whom do you interact most during the day, and what is the tone of those interactions? Are you engaging in community, or is your tendency to move toward isolation? Are your relationships marked by drama, stress, and conflict—or communication, enjoyment, and peace? What is your role in those interactions, and what steps can you take to have enriching interactions with the world around you?

The secret to emotional connection is becoming aware of who you are and what you are all about so that you are able to communicate that with the people closest to you. Once you've achieved awareness, the next step is to share that part of your life! Share your thoughts, your feelings, and your opinions with the people around you. Tell them about your emotions, your interactions, your goals and dreams.

All those little details are the things that make up the entirety of who you are. And as you express them, you offer another string that deepens the emotional connection between you and the people you love. But don't forget, it's just as important to give those strings as it is to be willing and ready to receive them. Make sure that you are also taking the time to ask questions and listen to your loved ones as they share their heart with you, building the intricate web of emotional connection with each and every interaction.

Sharing Your Interests

I saw an elderly husband and wife sitting together one morning at a coffee shop, and I promise you they looked like twins. They were eating and drinking the same food, wearing matching clothing, and even had an identical haircut. Something about this sweet couple, who seemed to share just about everything, made my heart melt. The emotional bond between them was so strong I could feel it halfway across the room. That was their secret: sharing everything. Not only the deepest parts of our hearts, as mentioned above, but everything else too. Developing a deep emotional bond comes with all the big strings of sharing your heart, coupled with all the little strings of sharing your interests. Both take time, which is why the season of summer is a season of connecting and cultivating.

If you want to take your emotional connection with someone to the next level, learn everything you can about things they love and why they love them. What are they interested in? What makes them tick? What do they enjoy? What are their favorites? And then—once you find out—start appreciating those things too, because every shared thing is another string of the elaborate and intricate web that holds you together.

When John and I were first getting to know each other, I took this idea to heart. When we first met, John was working at a research lab in Boston doing ophthalmology research. In other words, he was studying human eyes. Even though the thought of human eyeballs sent shivers down my spine (and still does), I remember spending hours online in the evenings, learning all about his research and trying to understand this career toward which he was moving. One evening when we were chatting on the phone, as we usually did to wrap up our day, I casually brought up the articles I had been reading, even though I probably understood about one in every ten words on the page. "Wait, you were reading about my research? That's so awesome!" That small act showed him that I wanted to connect. To this day, he jokes that he knew without a shadow of a doubt that I was either the biggest nerd ever, or that I was falling in love with him the moment I told him I was reading those scientific articles. He was right—about the latter part, anyway. Learning to love what he loved was another string in the web of emotional connection that we were building.

Learning to love what he loved was
another string in the web of emotional
connection that we were building.

To this day, we are spinning out strings to connect us to each other. A million little strings hold us together with the million little things we choose to share. That word "choose" is important because sharing interests and hobbies is not something that comes naturally for most people. That kind of sharing is something you have to choose to do. When you get into a relationship, you realize you are two different people with two different personalities, backgrounds, interests, tastes, and preferences. And, in a way, it should stay that way. This is not about becoming the same person. This is not about losing your identity and letting go of all that makes you unique. Being in relationship is about learning to share with one another and adding even more layers to your life than the ones that already existed. Relationships do not entail becoming a lesser version of yourself, but rather, a richer version of yourself.

Sharing Your Affection

What's the first thing that comes to mind when you hear the word "affection"? Is it romance? Sex? It is easy to connect the word "affection" with those things, but affection is not sexual in nature. The word "affection" refers to feelings of fondness toward someone. It communicates one very simple concept: "I like you." This is exactly why I chose to include it as the third pillar in building emotional connection. Affection is an emotion that starts coming to the surface in the season of summer because it is an emotion of exclusivity. It's not something you feel for anyone and everyone. Because of its exclusive nature, affection is a feeling that builds the strings of emotional connection in a powerful way.

Sharing your affection is an important part of building emotional intimacy and spinning your strings of connection. A lot of people "feel" affection toward someone on the inside but fail to express or convey that affection. This can cause confusion, hurt, and feelings of rejection. In a healthy relationship, as your affection for someone grows, your expression of that affection should also grow. Affection can be expressed through positive words: "Something I really appreciate about you is…" or through nonsexual touch, such as a hug, a hand on the back, or holding hands. Ultimately, a healthy display of affection allows you to express your fondness and communicate your care.

Emotional Protection

As important as it is to talk about emotional connection, we must also talk about its opposite: emotional protection. Once you start seeing emotional connection as the powerful web between you and someone else, you realize that it is something with which you have to be cautious, or you'll end up spinning strings of connection to the wrong people.

Suzy's Story

Suzy was a young woman who unknowingly started building a web of emotional connection with guys that weren't right for her. She had just moved to a new town, and she was feeling lonely and isolated. She was longing for emotional connection. Then she meets the guy next door. He's handsome. He's kind. And he wants to be her friend—with benefits. He was interested in hanging out, but more interested in their interactions afterward. Simply put, he wanted to have sex.

As a Christian, Suzy had previously decided that she didn't want to date or get in a relationship with someone who wasn't a believer. Not only that, she knew that sex was something sacred. But this relationship just seemed so convenient. In her loneliness, Suzy slowly began to let down her guard. Suzy and the guy next door started hanging out. They started going to the gym together, watching movies, and grabbing dinner. Quickly, their friendship started to escalate into something more, as the emotional strings began to grow thicker and thicker between them. She was investing a lot of time and energy in a relationship that wasn't good for her. Casual sex became a part of their interactions, and she soon started feeling stuck in the web of a relationship that she never expected for herself. Eventually, Suzy realized that the only way out was to start setting boundaries and protecting herself from further emotional connection.

Junk-Food Relationships

There's a reason junk food is so popular. It makes us feel good for a little while, it is quick, and most of all, it's convenient. But over time, it destroys our health and expands our waistline, and we ultimately end up regretting it. The same thing goes for "junk- food relationships." We all say we want healthy relationships, but in reality, most of us tend to go for what's easy and convenient rather than what's good for us.

Maybe for you it is not the guy next door but the girl at work who is easy to flirt with every day even though you know she is taken. Or that guy you met online with whom you've been texting hours into the night, even though he's starting to push the boundaries with inappropriate messages and sexual requests. Maybe it is that junk-food relationship you have with porn or with that guy or girl you've never actually interacted with but can't stop obsessing over in your head. It is easy to allow what's *convenient* to take the place of what's good in our lives, which is exactly why—whether we're single or married—we need to set up emotional boundaries as safeguards.

Protecting Your Interactions

One way we prevent the strings of emotional connection from happening is this: We don't connect. Connections cannot happen if we are not interacting. It's really as simple as that, but we tend to complicate it. Your interactions are one of the most important ways you show someone the value and role they have in your life. The more you choose to interact with someone (positive or even negative interactions), the more of yourself you are giving away, and the more you are "connecting." In a way, you have to learn to see your interactions as a commodity. They're a limited resource because you only have so much emotional energy to give each day. It is important to take inventory of to whom you are giving your interactions throughout the day, making sure to be deliberate about investing in the right people.

For those of us who are married, that means guarding our interactions with the opposite sex, making sure we're not building those intimate "emotional strings" with anyone other than our spouse. No one ever wakes up and says, "I think I'm going to destroy my marriage today." Destroying your relationship is a slow and steady process. An affair almost never starts with sex—it starts with one string and then another until the couple is so tightly connected they don't know how to detach themselves. Adultery-proofing your marriage means being aware of these strings from the very start. You have to be actively aware of the emotional strings you are building—and the emotional strings you are choosing *not* to build.

For those of you who are dating, being aware means taking a good look at the relationships in which you are getting emotionally connected. Are they the type of people who are building you up, encouraging you, and pointing you to Jesus? Are you investing in healthy relationships, or are you wasting your interactions on junk-food relationships?

Protecting Your Thoughts

So much of our relationships happen in our head. What I mean by that is that our thought life and our self-talk can really make or break how we're engaging in relationships. You attract the type of relationship you believe you deserve, so it is important to fill your mind with healthy, God-honoring truths about who you are and what your value is in Christ. What kind of relationships are you engaging in, and what do they say about the value you place on yourself? Understanding your value and learning to believe truth is an important part of protecting your thoughts and being proactive with the emotional connections you choose.

> You attract the type of relationship you believe you deserve, so it is important to fill your mind with healthy, God-honoring truths about who you are and what your value is in Christ.

Another part to protecting your thoughts is taking inventory of what you are allowing yourself to dwell on throughout the day. Are you living in a fantasy, or are you experiencing life in its reality?

Fantasy Versus Reality

I recently overheard two women discussing their fantasy boyfriends over coffee. They were chatting about their favorite "celebs," analyzing their hotness, what they love about them, why they would make amazing boyfriends, and how wonderful it would be to meet them face-to-face, or—better yet—to date them.

Another time, I listened to reporters on the news praise a pubescent teenager for asking his *Sports Illustrated* supermodel crush to come with him to prom.[7] How brave and courageous of him, they said. What an honorable thing to do in stepping out of his comfort zone and taking risks to engage his fantasies, they praised.

If you look around, you'll find that we live in a culture that is fixated on fantasy. We are so fixated on fantasy that it becomes the norm; it becomes our reality. Our imagined thought life becomes more real than the people and situations in front of us. I've actually heard people claim that they have literally "fallen in love" with celebrities, movie stars, porn stars, and supermodels. But the problem is that they are falling in love from a distance—falling in love with people that they don't actually know.

There is something safe about keeping people at a distance, obsessing over them from behind the sturdy walls of fantasy. There is something appealing about the unknown that makes it attractive, something about the mysterious that is seductive. Whether it's the supermodel on the cover of a magazine or that guy at work that you've never actually talked to, keeping people at a distance makes us desire them even more.

Keeping people at a distance is never messy. Loving from far away is never hard. It isn't mixed with the reality of pain, vulnerability, and selflessness; nor does it know the sacrifices of forgiveness and grace. But to really love, as C.S. Lewis says, is to be vulnerable: "There is no safe investment. To love at all is to be vulnerable. Love anything, and your heart will certainly be wrung and possibly be broken."[8] Real relationships with real people will always come with an element of mess.

So many men and women today are falling in love with a dream. They are falling in love with someone or something that doesn't really exist by taking the image of someone they don't actually know and giving them the character of who they want them to be. And that's exactly where unhealthy emotional ties begin to form.

This isn't just about crushing on Hollywood celebs, because fantasy can permeate many other parts of our life. Fantasy is living in what is not, rather than living in the reality of what actually is. In pornography, affairs, and toxic relationships, you will find men and women imprisoned within the confines of a dream. The married man glances at the beautiful office secretary, mentally engaging in a relationship with her, all the while forgetting her flaws and neglecting her deficits. The single woman analyzes and obsesses over a man she has hardly talked to, imagining what life could be if and when, only to have her heart broken by his lack of interest. The housewife is trapped in the fantasy and excitement of her romance novels, leaving her own reality behind instead of dealing with it. The young woman is stuck in an abusive marriage, making excuses and living for the dream of who he could be rather than acknowledging who he actually is and taking steps toward safety. The lonely young man spends hours every evening trapped by the pornographic images on his computer screen, growing numb to the beauty of real women and of real life. They are stuck in a life they make up with people who don't really exist. They have succumbed to a life fueled by fantasy rather than being grounded in reality. When fantasy becomes our reality, we may find we've fallen in love with a dream, fallen in love with an idea, but ultimately, fallen in love with a lie.

Choosing Reality

One of the keys to protecting ourselves from unhealthy emotional connections is to protect our minds by learning to live in reality. While there may be something provocative about living in a dream, there is something even more paralyzing about it.

When we live in a dream, we lose sight of what's real. We exchange our realities for something that can never actually exist. We live for what could be and end up missing what is. And in the end, we are led into disappointment, disillusionment, and destruction. We set ourselves up for failure by seeking to find a thing that doesn't actually exist, setting expectations that cannot be met by ourselves, much less anyone else.

When we live in a dream, we stop really living.

When we live in a dream, we stop really living.

Though they might not be as easy as Hollywood romance, real life and real relationships are well worth the investment. With the help of God's grace and our deliberate decisions, our real-life relationships can flourish into far greater than a simple dream because they can become our glorious reality.

If your reality is not what you had hoped it would be, it is time to make a change. Challenge yourself to learn and to grow, to forgive and mature, to heal and confess. Deal with things in your past, face the things in your present, and become the person you want to be. Don't live a passive life, but instead create a reality that you can be proud of by learning to build emotional ties with healthy people in healthy ways. The web of emotional connection is in your control.

Choose to connect with people who bring life, and protect yourself from all the others. And watch as your reality becomes even richer than your fantasy.

Reflection Questions for Couples

1. What are some practical things you can do to increase the strings of emotional connection in your marriage in each of these areas?

   a. Sharing your heart

   b. Sharing your interests

   c. Sharing your affection

2. When it comes to "emotional protection," are there any strings of connection that you need to cut out of your life in order to protect your marriage? How can you set boundaries to prevent those unhealthy emotional attachments from happening?

Reflection Questions for Singles

1. In what ways are you taking the initiative to build strings of emotional connection with healthy people in your life (friends, family, mentors)?

2. When it comes to "emotional protection," are there any junk-food relationships or unhealthy interactions you need to cut out of your life in order to protect your emotional and relational health?

3. When it comes to choosing "reality over fantasy," is there anything in your life that might be keeping you stuck on fantasy?

5

HEAT—SEXUAL CONNECTION

John and I were hanging out in his apartment one Sunday afternoon during the first few months of our dating relationship, and things were...shall we say...getting hot. "It's getting hot in here," he said. "Maybe we should step outside and go do something else." We did. It was the right choice.

Our friendship had officially moved into a dating relationship. We had walked through the season of spring with great strides and were now moving into the season of summer. Little by little, we were getting to know each other, building emotional connection and the strings that held us together. But as we shed the layers and continued revealing who we really were, we noticed that things quickly went from *warm* to *hot*. The affection we felt for one another was slowly starting to build into something a little trickier to navigate: sexual tension. We were drawn to each other sexually, and keeping our hands to ourselves turned out to be a much harder challenge than we expected. The heat of summer was starting to make us sweat.

In most romantic relationships, the heat of summer hits as soon as emotional connections begin to form. Physical attraction plus emotional connection equals sexual chemistry. For most dating couples, navigating their sexual attraction during dating is a complicated journey. This is especially true for Christians.

Growing up in the church, we are taught to see sex as a topic you don't really address before you are married. I recently asked my single readers at TrueLoveDates.com to tell me what messages they were taught about sex in church. Here's what they said:

"Sex is a gift to be celebrated in marriage, and that's about it."

"Don't do it, and don't even *speak* of it, until you are married."

"It's a hush-hush topic."

"It's taboo to talk about if you're married, and *really* taboo if you're single."

"Refrain from sex and seek sainthood if you're single."

"It's the great big apple God gave us and then said, 'Don't touch it!'"

How many of us can relate to some of those messages that may have been passed down to us as well? So often in Christian circles, we treat sex like a "say no to drugs" campaign, and then somehow, we are supposed to magically figure out how to navigate it with success, joy, and ultimate pleasure when the time comes.

Unfortunately, that is not how things tend to happen. I've heard from a lot of men and women who are going into marriage confused as to what to expect when it comes to sex. They are having a hard time shifting their thinking from seeing sex through a negative lens their entire lives to suddenly seeing it as good, holy, and special. This shift in thinking doesn't always come easy, especially when no one is talking much about it. Our silence has allowed for false expectations to develop and has left many men and women to try to figure it all out on their own. As a professional counselor, I work with many couples who are struggling with sex in their marriage and feel like they have nowhere to turn. It is time for the church to become a safe place where we can bring all our struggles and be welcomed with open arms and open conversations.

Let's Talk About Sex

If you come from a Christian community or family, "Let's talk about sex" is probably not an invitation you hear often. In fact, I've heard from too many young men and women who feel as though sex is not something that is talked about often enough within the context of faith and spirituality. The conversation about sex is one that is missing from the Christian community, as though not talking about it will magically make it go away. That underlying belief is a huge part of the problem.

> The conversation about sex is one that is missing from the Christian community, as though not talking about it will magically make it go away.

By not saying anything about sex, we're saying something. We're saying that sex is a topic that is not supposed to be discussed. And in the silence, our views of sex and sexuality begin to be shaped and molded by culture and society, yet without a clear gauge of what is healthy or good.

It is time to talk about sex because while we don't, others are. All around us, people are telling us about sex. Turn on any TV station, tune in to any radio station, or open any magazine, and you'll be bombarded by images and messages that speak to you about what sex is. The world tells us that sex is about pleasure and passion, or that it is a tool, used to get what you want in life. The world tells us that sex is an antidote to make you feel good when you are down. It is an instrument, selfishly used to get love and to feel intimacy. Our concept of sex is being distorted by lust rather than love, by casual encounters rather than commitment. It is time to speak up about sex because our silence is allowing others to speak for us.

> It is time to speak up about sex because our silence is allowing others to speak for us.

Sex Is Good

One of the biggest problems with the dialogue (or the lack thereof) that we've created around sex is that our conversations are rooted in so much guilt and shame. All throughout our lives, we are inadvertently (sometimes not so inadvertently) told that sex is bad, wrong, and shameful. We're bombarded by messages about the harm of sex before marriage but without being told enough of its beauty within marriage, and then we unintentionally carry these largely negative messages into life and into marriage.

Sex is good! Sex is a gift. It is important for us to stop referring to sex simply as something to be avoided, and instead, take the time to bring balance to the truth that it is worth saying "yes" to sex done in God's way. We need to hear less about why it is wrong and more about why (and when) it is right.

Sex is God's gift to us, and when we talk about it the right way, it brings Him glory. Our culture has done so much harm to this gift by using it and abusing it through the pornography industry, sex trafficking, abuse, addictions, and the like. Our media has misconstrued it to reflect lust and selfishness. God's design for sex has been misused, degraded, and perverted. But God is longing to redeem sex because it belongs to Him! It was His idea, and it is something that He created to bring Him glory. God delights in His children, and He longs for us to experience this gift at its best, as it was made to be enjoyed.

An Attitude of Gratitude

I'll never forget the time I sat across from my mentor at a booth in Applebee's one Sunday afternoon in college. I had just finished sharing with her about some of the sexual struggles I was facing in my dating relationship at the time. After pouring out my heart, I sat there, waiting for her to give me the lecture I deserved. Her response not only surprised me, but paved the way for healing in my life.

"Deb, be grateful for those sexual desires! Thank God for them!"

Wait, grateful? Did I hear that right? I was waiting to get some Bible verses tossed my way, a five-step action plan toward recovery, increased accountability time, or a nice, big serving of guilt and shame. So, it took me a moment to realize that my ears weren't deceiving me.

"Those desires were placed in you by God, and they're going to come in handy someday. We need to thank God that He loves us enough to allow us to experience sexual desires, and then we need to trust that His plan for how we should fulfill those desires is best."

That shift in perspective removed so much shame and brought me freedom, and that freedom gave me the motivation I needed to commit to doing things in God's way and in God's time. The first step to overcoming sexual struggles starts by having a healthy perspective of sexual desires. We need to be *grateful* for the desires God has given us. Shame leads to more struggle, but gratitude leads to healing.

> Shame leads to more struggle,
> but gratitude leads to healing.

A friend of mine shared with me that as his three sons were getting to the age where sexual desires and struggles were starting to become commonplace, he would always remind them of the power of gratitude. He'd say, "Learn to thank God for sexual pleasure, whether in a dream, holding hands, a first kiss, whenever. And if you can't thank God for it, don't do it. Your conscience is a poor guide because culture influences conscience. But gratitude can be used by the Spirit to direct you."

"Your conscience is a poor guide." The truth in that little statement has the power to bring so much freedom to our lives. Our conscience is fickle. It changes based on what we've read, to whom we've talked, how much sleep we've had, and what we've watched that day. But gratitude can be used by the Spirit to help us know right from wrong, and to give us the motivation to trust that God's way is best for our lives. That's why it is so important to start this conversation within the framework that sex and sexual desires are good. They are a gift from God—a gift that He wants us to enjoy to the fullest! And that is why we must learn to be stewards of this gift, so that we can enjoy it in the right time and in the right way.

Sex Is Powerful

Did you ever wonder why we are told that sex is best within the framework of marriage? In working with singles and couples alike, I advocate for sex only in the context of marriage because I see its power.

Sex Is Binding

More powerful than a kiss and more intimate than an embrace is the emotional intimacy that is experienced within the walls of sexual intimacy. We have to talk about this component when we talk about sex because sex is meant to amplify emotional intimacy. When you have sex, feel-good chemicals are being released in your body. The main chemical, oxytocin, is also called the "bonding chemical," and is the exact same chemical that is released when a mother is nursing her baby. With or without your awareness, this chemical is giving you an extra bond, a deeper connection to the person you are with—whether or not that relationship is good for you.

This is an absolutely beautiful and important thing within the context of a marriage, gluing your hearts, bodies, and souls together. But an unfortunate thing occurs when sex is used the other way around—as a way to bind two people who haven't committed to each other.

Sex before marriage is like a fake commitment in that it fuels a false sense of emotional intimacy and attachment outside the commitment of a permanent relationship. But, real or fake, when it comes to intimacy, it is nearly impossible for our brain to separate the physical and emotional components of sex. They are dependent on each other, and they work together. Whether or not we are even aware, our perceptions and interactions within a relationship are impacted by sex. This is great news for those of us who are married. But for those who are not, sexual intimacy before a marital commitment can cause confusion and majorly mess with our emotional compass by fooling us into thinking we have a depth to our relationship that is not backed up by commitment.

It is nearly impossible for our brain to separate
the physical and emotional components of sex.

Not only that, but our sexual experiences before marriage actually set the stage for what we expect in marriage. We are creatures of habit, and our sexual experiences become a part of our expectations, insecurities, needs, desires, feelings, and fears. Our sexual experiences before marriage directly affect our ability to enjoy sex in that we are shaping our sexual palette with each action and interaction—because we end up desiring what we get used to.

Our expectations and desires are impacted in a profound way by the intensity and frequency of sexual experiences before marriage and can cause major disappointment and problems after marriage. We cannot have the conversation about sex without explaining that sex and psychology go hand in hand.

Sex Is Healing

Sex was designed to make you feel good. Have you ever heard of the term "make-up sex"? That's essentially referring to the idea that after a big fight or argument, people tend to have really good sex because it is one of the ways in which they feel close and connected to make up for the negative experience or conflict that made them feel disconnected. Sex is "healing" in that it makes you feel like everything is okay and fills in the missing pieces. In marriage, this tends to be a really important aspect of sex, offering you one more tool toward intimacy, restoration, and reconciliation with this person to whom you've committed your life.

But outside of the context of marriage, sex can "heal" things that were never meant to be healed. In many cases, sex outside of marriage is an instrument that is used to actually cover relationship flaws instead of dealing with them. Roger Hillerstrom compares a couple's relationship before marriage to a steam pipe.[1] The main job of a steam pipe is to transport pressure. If you think about it, a relationship is filled with pressure—from how you connect to how you communicate, from your conflict style to your emotional temperament, from your personality differences to your individual lifestyle, from your family of origin issues to your past baggage. All those things create pressure in a relationship, and that's a really good thing. Pressure helps you understand what the relationship is all about. But just like steam pipes, relationships are prone to have cracks and flaws. When pressure builds in a steam pipe, it begins to reveal the cracks and flaws because you can finally get a glimpse of where the steam is spilling out. That tells you where the steam pipe needs to be repaired, and whether or not it's even strong enough to survive. But when that pressure is being released through a different means (in this analogy, through sex outside of marriage), the cracks are never found or realized. Eventually, those very cracks are the things that end up destroying a relationship.

Every relationship must undergo a series of pressures in order to see whether or not it will stand the test of time. When sex becomes a part of a dating relationship, it instantly begins to cover up those relationship flaws, and oftentimes leads you to stay in a relationship far longer than you should—whether or not the relationship can be repaired, whether or not it's even strong enough to survive the test of time, the test of lifelong commitment. Outside of marriage, sex is like the Novocain of relationships, numbing you to what's really going on in the relationship.

Sex Is a Symptom

So why is it that even though we can logically talk through the significant effects of sex outside of marriage, it is still so prevalent in our society today? There's no better way to explain it than to say that sex is a symptom. It's a symptom of something far deeper than we often realize. Sex is rooted in our underlying need and desire as human beings for one thing and one thing alone: connection. Sex is a sign of our deep need to connect.

It is no coincidence that when a married couple is connected emotionally and spiritually, their sex life improves by leaps and bounds. It is also no coincidence that when singles are plugged into community and are connected emotionally and spiritually, they can manage their sex drive so much more effectively. The greater our level of positive, meaningful, life-giving connection, the healthier we'll be in all areas of our life, including our sex life.

The greater our level of positive, meaningful,
life-giving connection, the healthier we'll be
in all areas of our life, including our sex life.

We don't often see it that way, but that is exactly what's happening behind the scenes. In the moment, it seems like sex is about sex. We have feelings, desires, and physical reactions happening in our bodies. But sex is not just about sex; it's about connection. Sex reveals a longing for something greater and a desire for something deeper.

I Want More

The first time I truly grasped this reality was when I met Amanda. I was a new counselor, fresh out of grad school, and she was one of my very first clients. When she walked into my office, I was bursting at the seams with my novice optimism, pencil in hand, ready to jot down notes and change the world. "Good morning, Amanda!" I said, with the cheesiest smile she's likely ever seen, "How can I help you today?" Looking back, her somber voice and flat affect were clear giveaways that I was totally unprepared for what I was about to hear. With very little facial expression and absolutely no tears, she quietly told me her story. She was caught in a trap of sexual experiences with toxic men. One after the other, she was sleeping with men who treated her poorly and abandoned her easily. But she just couldn't figure out how to stop.

Over the next few months and years, Amanda found a special place in my heart. I had the unique privilege of hearing the details of her difficult story. When she was only a child, Amanda witnessed her mother be brutally murdered in her own home at the hands of her stepdad. After that ordeal, her biological father tried to step in to care for her, but he was battling his own demons, which caused him to be distant and emotionally unavailable. They barely spoke, and they hardly interacted. They were two shadows living in the same house. So, without connection with her mother and the emotional presence of her father, Amanda found herself feeling completely and utterly alone at the tender age of 12. Shortly after that, Amanda began to unconsciously seek out connection with just about anyone she could find. She started having sex at the young age of 13, and the connection she experienced felt like a drug. It gave her a false sense of intimacy—something she had been longing for her entire life. Sex became her drug, numbing her to what was really going on in her life.

I worked with Amanda for many years. I'm so proud to say that little by little, everything about this young twentysomething woman began to change. I watched her transform from the inside out as she began to understand her deep need for connection and what it meant to fill that need in a healthy way. She started understanding her true value, her deep worth, and believing that she deserved more than she was experiencing. Her addiction to sex began to lose its grip on her life. Because sex wasn't really about sex. Sex was about something far deeper. Sex was about experiencing connection—connection to self, connection to others, and most importantly, connection to God. Believe it or not, eventually my cheesy grin was met with a cheesy grin of her own as she walked into my office. Her flat affect was replaced by one of the most beautiful smiles I have ever seen—the reflection of a life that had been transformed by the work of Jesus Christ. Her life had finally felt connected to something bigger, to someone greater.

> Sex wasn't really about sex. Sex was about something far deeper. Sex was about experiencing connection—connection to self, connection to others, and most importantly, connection to God.

We All Come with a Price Tag

Moments like the one I had with Amanda remind me that we all come with a price tag. We all live life with an unspoken value that we place on ourselves—a value that impacts how we choose to live and what's worth living for. That value determines how we do relationships and how we view sex.

One evening, I was on a walk with a prostitute. I was involved in an ongoing ministry to people in a specific inner-city location, and we had become good friends over time. That evening, I had pulled into the street to make some visits and happened to see her camped out on the street corner, looking for some business. I got out of the car and walked over to her, and we started to chat. I'm not much for small talk, so I quickly got right to the point. I knew she had been working at letting go of this particular "occupation," and so I wondered what she was doing here today.

"Hey...what's going on?" I said, straight to the point.

She looked down at the ground and replied, "Well, I'm in another bind, and it's a way to make some quick money."

I don't remember too many details of our conversation that evening, but there is one thing she said through the course of our talk that I will likely never forget because it made my stomach churn, my heart sink, and my spirit ache:

"Fifty bucks is real good money."

I recall having a conversation with another young woman. She had been sexually involved with a guy who had now cheated on her. But the problem was, they were never even dating to begin with. Their interactions in friendship started crossing the emotional and physical lines, until one thing led to another. Shortly after that, they were regularly having sex and fooling around, with no commitment, no conversation, and no real relationship. She came to chat with me after four months of this "relationship" left her with a broken heart and a broken sense of self.

I can't help but see a theme that connects these stories. Two different women from totally different parts of the country, from different socioeconomic statuses, different races, and different ages. But they had one thing in common: They each came with a price tag—a value they placed on themselves that determined how they lived, how they engaged in relationships, and even how they viewed sex.

But don't we all?

If we are honest with ourselves, we will realize that this one very important truth is actually reflected in how we live our lives. It may be a literal price tag, like the prostitute's cost of a one-night stand, but it may also be an emotional price tag. Either way, it is a price tag that we each place on ourselves based on *what we believe we deserve.*

No matter how we look at it, there is no getting around the fact that the giving of ourselves will *always* come at a cost. Whenever we choose to engage in any kind of relationship, there is always some sort of cost involved. It will cost us our heart, our spirit, our bodies, and our minds. It will cost our emotions, our time, our commitment, and our energy.

We always come with a price tag, and we will value ourselves with the price tag that we believe we deserve. Even more sobering is the reality that we will likely be "purchased" at the price that we place on ourselves. If you believe you are worth a measly $50 or an ambiguous relationship that revolves only around sex, that is usually what you will get.

The most difficult truth is that there are some men and women who set their price tag so low because they are desperately looking for love, desperately looking for connection. But when we are easy to purchase, we'll also be easy to replace.

My heart goes out to every man and woman who has ever believed that they were worth less than they are. My heart goes out to every man and woman who has ever allowed their heart to be wounded, broken, and bruised at the hands of someone who didn't see the value that they truly possessed.

Child of God, no matter who you are or what you've been through, you are worth so much more than what you believe you deserve. You have been purchased by a God who saw that you were worth far more than you ever could have imagined, and so He bought you at a high cost just to prove it. You were purchased by the blood of Jesus, by a God who gave His very Son so that you could have a sense of your value, security, and worth. He did this so that you could hold your head up high, so that you could believe that you are magnificent and remarkable.

Child of God, no matter who you are or what
you've been through, you are worth so much
more than what you believe you deserve.

Child of God, it's time for you to rise up and claim the price at which you've been purchased (1 Corinthians 6:20). It's time to recognize that your price has been set high, and that you are worthy of someone who sees the divine value given to you by the God who makes all things beautiful. It's time to say "no" to lies that degrade your body, invalidate your emotions, and muffle your voice, making you feel small and insignificant. What you believe about yourself will always determine how you live and the type of relationships you believe you deserve. We all come with a price tag. It's time to start believing that you are worth so much more.

Sex at Its Best

I could end this chapter with a list of reasons why you shouldn't have sex before marriage. I could write a whole chapter about the dangers of premarital sex and list the physical and emotional consequences of sexually transmitted diseases and sexual struggles. I could give you a chart outlining "how far is too far," some suggestions for practical boundaries, and talk you through the dangers of getting stuck in the season of summer when you choose to allow sex to be a part of your relationship before marriage.

But all of that has been said and done, and you can find plenty of great books on those topics. But as I look at my personal journey and understanding of sex, one of the things that has been most motivating to me is not the reasons why I *shouldn't* have sex before marriage (though there are many), but the reasons why I *should* save sex for marriage. When I could finally see sex in marriage as God's *best* plan for my life, it started shifting something in me. I was able to dig deep and find true motivation for the wait. I saw marriages around me crumbling, and I wanted my future marriage to be the best it could possibly be. I began to see waiting as more than simply saying "no" to something I wanted now; instead, I saw it as an incredible investment for later.

Married sex gets a really bad rap in our society. They tell you that once you get married, your sex life gets boring and eventually becomes nonexistent. But if you ask me, that misrepresentation of marital sex is not only misleading, it is a lie from the pit of hell. Satan's scheme is to get men and women to have as much sex as they can before marriage, and as little as possible after marriage. Many of us have bought into this lie, and in turn, our relational lives have suffered great consequences. But if we could truly believe that God's intention is for us to enjoy sex in its most glorious form, it would begin to change our perspective, and in turn, change our approach.

Why Marital Sex Is Best

The beautiful thing about sex is that it is not actually about the sex; it is about something so much bigger and greater and more meaningful. Marital sex is about a constant connection with another human being throughout the journey of life. The beauty of marital sex is that it is not only about the heat of the moment; it is about the significance of day-to-day moments, from a special look to a special touch. From an act of service to an opportunity for selflessness. From unloading the dishwasher to speaking an encouraging word. Marital sex is about choice after choice that may start with the mundane but leads to an intimate experience later on that night. This deep psychological connection between two people who *truly* know, love, serve, and sacrifice for one another spills out into sex and turns it into something more meaningful than anything Hollywood can muster.

Another thing Hollywood certainly doesn't tell you is that married sex is one of those things that gets better over time. I was just talking to a friend who said the exact same thing about her relationship with her husband. Yet for those of us who are truly enjoying married sex, I'm sure we could all acknowledge that for most of us, it definitely didn't start there. It took time to develop the necessary emotional and communication skills. There is so much about ourselves and about one another that we each need to actively and deliberately learn along the way. Just like anything worthwhile in life, a deep and meaningful sexual relationship takes time, effort, and a whole lot of practice. The beauty of marital sex as God intended for it to be is that there's no rush; there's only time—a lifetime, to be exact. Plenty of time to learn, to grow, to savor, and to enjoy sex in the safety of commitment.

Our culture likes to brainwash us into believing that the hottest sex is illicit sex with different partners. That underlying message is portrayed in our media, in our entertainment, and even in our commercials. Our culture also perpetuates the stereotype that, for married couples, sex gets boring and needs to be supplemented by ever-increasing deviance; hence, the need for handcuffs, whips, ropes, pornography, and *50 Shades of Grey*. But those who constantly need "bigger and better" things will never be capable of getting their fill. Our sexual appetites are not meant to control us; we are meant to control them. The truth is, there is a *deep* level of pleasure within the security of the familiar. To know and be known is one of life's most amazing gifts. Within the familiarity of marriage, we are more than free to try new things, but we are also free to enjoy the same things again and again. Within the familiarity of marriage, there's an openness in asking, in experimenting, and even in saying, "No thanks." Gone are the worries to have to "look perfect" or to "be an expert" because within the familiarity of a healthy marriage, you are already known, already loved, already desired, and already accepted just as you are. A one-night stand cannot possibly compare with this kind of depth.

With all this in mind, allow me to take it one step further and remind you of the deep spiritual connection that happens when two people become one in sex. Sex does not just put two bodies together physically, but also spiritually. When two people have sex, there is a supernatural union that happens on a deep level. The beauty of sex within the framework of a loving, committed, God-honoring marriage is that there is a love present that surpasses all understanding because it's not of this world. This love points to nothing other than the incredible, life-giving, and ferocious love of Jesus Christ. And when the unconditional love of God is found between two people, it overflows into their hearts, into their marriage, and into their bedroom. The truth is, the more the love, the better the sex because unconditional love between two people is the greatest turn-on imaginable.

Navigating the Heat of Summer

If you are reading this chapter as someone who is single, my prayer is that this would encourage you and motivate you to continue waiting—or even to begin waiting—for marriage, no matter what your sexual history. Consider the value of sexual intimacy within marriage, not only the dangers of premarital sex. Consider the work that God is doing in you and through you as you trust in Him. The pleasures of marital sex done in God's way and in God's time are worth the wait. But sexual fulfillment doesn't simply come from waiting until marriage. It comes with choosing the right spouse—someone who will join you on this important emotional, spiritual, and psychological journey. The right spouse is someone you can trust and someone with whom you can feel safe. And part of the process of choosing the right person is becoming the right person.

If you are reading this chapter as someone who is married, I pray that you would be at a place in your relationship that you can give a heartfelt "AMEN!" as you read through these words. But some of you aren't where you desire to be when it comes to your sexual relationship. Maybe this chapter has challenged you to take a couple steps back and make some things right, whether emotionally, spiritually, or psychologically between you and your spouse. Maybe it's brought some things up that you've not wanted to deal with for some time. Maybe you've felt convicted or maybe even inspired. There are so many barriers that keep us from a fulfilling sex life in the way that God intends. It is important to be learning about sex, praying about sex, and intentionally opening the doors of dialogue with your spouse in order to take the next steps and make the season of summer the best that it can possibly be in your relationship. Please be sure to reference the endnotes of this chapter for some additional resources to help you get there.[2]

For others, this chapter may have triggered some deep hurts from past wounds or experiences. Whether because of sexual addiction, infidelity, or abuse and trauma, maybe your picture of sex (either in or out of marriage) has come with painful wounds and memories. If you have been a victim in some way, I want you to know that God's heart breaks for you! God hates these things even more than you do because He knows how much pain sin brings into the lives of His people. If you haven't already, I challenge you to find a Christian professional counselor to get started on your own journey of healing. There is so much hope for the future, even in the face of a broken past. Don't wait for "the other person" to change or to heal; instead, begin that journey for yourself right here and right now.

Just as with the heat of a fire, the heat of sex in the season of summer can either destroy your relationship or sustain it with its flames. It is up to you to determine how you will use its power. May God give you the strength, the endurance, and the determination to wield it well.

Reflection Questions for Couples

1. What voices, influences, and conversations have shaped and continue to shape your view of sex?

2. Do you carry any negative views of sex into your marriage relationship? If yes, how might those views of sex be impacting your relationship?

3. "The greater our level of positive, meaningful, life-giving connection, the healthier we'll be in all areas of our life, including our sex life." With that idea in mind, what are some practical steps you can take toward becoming a healthier person?

4. Are you enjoying "married sex at its best"? If not, what are some practical steps you and your spouse can take together to enjoy and enhance your sexual relationship?

Reflection Questions for Singles

1. What voices, influences, and conversations have shaped and continue to shape your view of sex?

2. Do you carry any negative views of sex? If yes, how can you begin the process of rewriting those views?

3. In this chapter, I argue that sex is binding and healing, but in the wrong context the power of sex can build unhealthy bonds between two people. How can you set boundaries to keep your heart, body, and mind from unhealthy physical or sexual connections?

6

FIRE—SPIRITUAL INTIMACY

s it hot in here? Or is that just the Holy Spirit burning inside of you?"

Every now and again, I start my seminars for singles with a list of outrageous Christian pickup lines. If you've ever heard me speak at a church, marriage conference, college, or singles event, you know my tendency as a counselor is to go deep fast. Which is why I always like to start with something a little on the lighter side. I figure it's only fair to laugh together before we cry together.

And I honestly know of few things funnier than Christian pickup lines. In case you are taking notes, here are some of my favorites (Caution: Use at your own risk.):

- "Hi, I'm Will. God's Will" (wink, wink). P.S. I suggest your name actually be Will if you're going to try this one out. No need to start a relationship on lies.

- "I didn't believe in predestination—until tonight!"

- "So, I was reading the book of Numbers last night when I realized I don't have yours!"

- "I'm usually not very prophetic, but I can see us together."

- "I'm a Proverbs 32 kind of guy, and you're a Proverbs 31 kind of girl."

- "How many times do I have to walk around you to make you fall for me?"

- "Is it a sin you stole my heart?"

- "Is your name Faith? Because you're the substance of the things I've hoped for!"

- "Want to practice speaking in tongues with me?" (Okay, maybe this one isn't such a good idea.)

The fact that Christian pickup lines even exist suggests to me that people are looking to lead into relationships with faith. For people of faith, faith is an important part of the ingredients necessary for making a relationship work, and rightly so. Over the years, many scientific studies have pointed to the idea that people with a strong connection to religion have been linked to lower divorce rates and higher marital satisfaction.[1] Not only that, but one specific study found that couples with *shared* faith and beliefs about God and marriage reported greater marital adjustment, less conflict, better communication, and an increased ability to push through problems in their relationship.[2] The more a couple had in common regarding their spiritual beliefs and practices, the better they functioned in their marriage and the higher satisfaction they experienced in their relationship. Science points to what Scripture already tells us: Mutual faith in God holds a relationship together, and being equally yoked really matters.

Equally Yoked

If you've grown up in the church, you've likely heard the term "equally yoked." This phrase is taken from 2 Corinthians 6:14, which says, "Do not be yoked together with unbelievers. For what do righteousness and wickedness have in common? Or what fellowship can light have with darkness?" Usually, this passage is shared in the context of explaining that when it comes to romantic relationships, we need to make sure we are in a relationship with someone who identifies as a Christian. I think there's so much value in that interpretation of Scripture, but I'd like to take this analogy just a little bit deeper because I think we sell ourselves short of healthy relationships by not looking at the big picture of the context of this passage.

When talking about being "yoked together" in 2 Corinthians, Paul is using a farming metaphor. In order to grasp this analogy to its fullest, you have to understand some of the intricacies of farming culture. Living in the Amish town of Lancaster, PA, and interacting with farmers on a regular basis, I've learned a lot more about farming and agriculture than I ever could have imagined. In fact, the founding pastor of my home church, Pastor Sam, is very open about his background as a former Amish man, and what it was like growing up in a world of agriculture and farming, but without the luxuries of modern technology. Given his history, I decided he would be the perfect person to ask about what it meant to be equally yoked in terms of farming.

He explained that the idea of "yoking" is essentially pairing two animals together in order to prepare them for the work of plowing. The yoke was the solid wooden structure that would hold the pair of animals together. Now, when it comes to yoking two animals, it's a no-brainer that you are going to pair two of the same type of animal. Two mules, two horses, etc. Two different animals would never work together in a setting like this. But not only that, the farmer's job was to try and yoke together the two animals that were also the best fit.

According to Pastor Sam, "For a team to work well together, they had to pull together, and both pull their share of the load. Sometimes, we would buy a team of mules, and they didn't work well together. So, we had to go buy another mule for the team. My dad would always examine them to see their strength, disposition, and personality." Just let that truth sink in for a moment. A good team has to be compatible in their strength, their disposition, and their personality. They had to be matched based on their ability to pull—*together*. Pastor Sam went on to say, "If they aren't teamed well, we wouldn't get as much accomplished in the field because we'd have to stop and spend time adjusting their yoke." If one animal is weaker than the other, the weak one will hold the strong one back. Because of the lack of balance, they will have to work much harder but without the reward.

On the other hand, a team that is equally yoked is worth its weight in gold. Pastor Sam told me about his prize mules: "We had a pair of mules that were the best in the whole community. They would never give up when pulling something. When they were not working, they were the best of friends. They would always stand side by side in the meadow, oftentimes stroking each other." They were side by side even when they didn't have to be, when nothing was holding them together. To me, that is a picture of a beautiful relationship. We sure can learn a lot from mules.

This is why I am adamant that the idea of being equally yoked is so much more meaningful and revolutionary than we realize. We're not just asked to be in relationship with someone claiming to be a Christian like us. We need to find someone who matches us spiritually in their strength, their disposition, and their personality. We need someone who loves God the way we love God, who prioritizes their relationship with Jesus the way we prioritize ours. The person who exudes the fruit of the Holy Spirit at work in their life the way we exude it in ours is the one we want. We want someone who is similarly committed to God and is ready and willing to do the good, hard work of the kingdom of God. This is not just about marrying a Christian. This is about being matched together with someone who is wholly committed to plowing through life with you—the good, the bad, and the ugly of life—by your side, hand in hand, moving in God's direction, even when there's nothing but their vows keeping them there. Not only is it important to look for someone like that, it's crucial that we *become* someone like that because our team will only be as strong as the weakest link.

The Fire of the Spirit of God

I started this chapter with a funny pick-up line, asking, "Is it hot in here or is that just the Holy Spirit burning inside of you?" I meant that to be humorous, of course, but there's more truth to that statement than we might first realize. All throughout Scripture, the word "fire" is used to depict the power and presence of God and the Holy Spirit. In Luke 3:16, John the Baptist tells the people, "I baptize you with water. But one who is more powerful than I will come, the straps of whose sandals I am not worthy to untie. He will baptize you with the Holy

Spirit and fire." In the book of Acts, the disciples experienced what seemed to be "tongues of fire" that descended on them as the Holy Spirit came and rested upon each one of them (Acts 2:3-4). In Exodus 19:18 we read that "Mount Sinai was covered with smoke because the LORD descended on it in fire."

One of the most important aspects of the season of summer is to take inventory of the level of spiritual fire exuding from your relationship. The fire of God at work in your life is what fuels your love and, in turn, fuels your relationship. Friends, if you hear nothing else, hear this: The fire of God's Spirit is the one and only thing that will continue to fan the flame of your love when the warmth of your emotions has diminished and the heat of your sexual connection has waned. Summer love will only continue to grow and spread if its fire is coming from the only source that never dies out—the unquenchable fire of the unconditional love of God. When our relationships are rooted in that kind of love, nothing can stop us: "For love is as strong as death… it burns like a blazing fire, like a mighty flame" (Song of Solomon 8:6).

> The fire of God's Spirit is the one and only thing that will continue to fan the flame of your love when the warmth of your emotions has diminished and the heat of your sexual connection has waned.

Fueling the Fire in Dating

"We just started dating a few weeks ago, but we're really trying to keep Jesus at the center of our relationship," he said to me.

I'm always grateful for a chance to talk to people face-to-face after I speak somewhere, so I was glad when this young college student came up to chat with me after my relationship seminar was over. He continued: "So, in order to do that, we're reading a daily devotional together and praying together every day."

"Hmm," I said.

The look on my face, the tone of my "hmm," and the abruptness of my answer probably said more than I had hoped to say.

"Is that not what you would suggest?" he asked sincerely.

"To be honest, I commend your desire to make Jesus the center of your relationship. That is *such* a good thing! But I struggle with the thought that a daily devotional is going to get you there. And praying together, well, that is such an intimate thing. In this early stage of dating, I don't recommend that you combine your spiritual lives just yet. There is a deep power in spiritual intimacy, and the best thing you can do for your relationship is to keep investing in your individual relationship with God, and then see how that impacts your relationship."

I advocate moving slowly in terms of spiritual connection when you are in a dating relationship because there are few things more intimate than a spiritual connection. Some couples get spiritually exclusive way too soon. They end up going too deep, too fast by praying together, doing their devotions together, and ultimately bonding spiritually long before they've committed emotionally. In an effort to "do things right" in their relationship, they jump into the deep end by sharing a spiritual connection before their commitment has reached that level of intimacy. I met another young woman who was completely devastated after dating a guy for only two months because they had shared a deep spiritual connection right from the start rather than waiting for a deeper commitment.

Just as with other aspects of your relationship, it is important to make sure that your spiritual relationship is growing proportionally to your level of commitment.

Play Together—Don't Pray Together

Don't pray together? It might sound contradictory to your Christian beliefs. We've always been taught that prayer is such an important part of any relationship. I know of so many couples who started their relationship by investing time in deep spiritual prayer with one another and spending time in God's Word together. While this sounds well and good, in my opinion, it's actually a really dangerous road to travel in the early stages of a relationship.

Seeking the heart of God and pouring out your heart and soul to Him through prayer is one of the most emotionally vulnerable things you will ever do. It is essentially like being spiritually naked before God because you hide nothing emotionally. It is so important to pray about your relationship and to seek God's voice, but *wait* to seek it together. In the early stages of dating, seek to pursue God as an individual before allowing your relationship with Him to become a trio prematurely by including your significant other. There will be a day for deep and intimate spiritual unity, but it is not now.

Your dating relationship in its early stages is meant to be a time of getting to know each other and learning all the superficial things you can know before taking it to the next level. Use this season for that. Don't go too deep too fast because the spiritual intimacy that comes with deep shared moments like this can pull you in far deeper than you were ever meant to go and, in the end, leave you with a broken heart—and a broken spirit.

Make Room for the Spirit

I went to a Christian college, and when two people were caught hugging for a couple seconds too long, some pesky onlooker was bound to yell out, "Make room for the Spirit!" How does a couple make room for the Spirit during dating without getting too spiritually intimate? The best advice I have for you is the same thing I told the young man earlier in this chapter: Continue to fuel the fire of God in your own life as an individual. Make space for the Holy Spirit to be alive and at work in how you live your life on a daily basis. Fueling the fire of the Spirit in your relationship means fueling the power of the Spirit in your own life first and foremost because that fire will impact everything it touches—including your dating relationship.

Maybe that means making literal space in your life—reducing the noise, turning off Netflix for a while, monitoring your time on social media. Making space for the Holy Spirit might mean getting busy memorizing Scripture, allowing God's Word to sink into the deepest parts of who you are. Or perhaps it will mean finding a spiritual mentor to help you identify areas of spiritual strength you need to expand

and weaknesses on which you need to work. It could mean spending time in God's Word rather than spending every moment with your boyfriend or girlfriend. Whatever it means for you, the bottom line is that learning to fuel the fire of God in your own life will ultimately reap great rewards in your relationship. This doesn't mean you don't talk about God or share what He's doing in your life. Because when you are connected to Jesus, there's going to be—and *should* be—a natural over-flow of that love in every part of your life. Aim to fuel the fire of God in your personal life, and then watch and see what happens. Because God's fire sets ablaze everything it touches, including you.

Fueling the Fire in Marriage

The very things we are ecstatic about doing before marriage tend to be the very things that lose their luster after marriage. The same couple who was so quick to get a couple's devotional the moment they started dating are the very same ones who find that devotional gathering dust in some random drawer after marriage. The same madly-in-love college students dying to hold hands and pray are now the very same drained and exhausted parents of two young babies, pinching themselves just to stay awake during their prayers before bed.

That is why it is so important for the fire of God to be an integral part of our lives, not just some random practices or traditions we try to sprinkle on our relationship in hopes that it will keep our marriage "God-centered."

Remember Your First Love

Nothing we do can center our relationship on God more than centering our individual hearts on God. But it is so easy to lose our first love, isn't it? It is easy to somehow get so lost in the grind of life, marriage, parenting, and career that our first love gets moved to the back of the line. The deep love of God loses its luster. The fierce grace that once radically changed our lives becomes familiar. It is easy for the extraordinary to become ordinary when we are used to having it every day. But you and I are not the first ones to struggle with this.

In the book of Revelation, we see this struggle playing out in the early church of Ephesus. They started well. They seemed like they had it together on the outside. They worked hard. They persevered through hard times. Their life was marked by good works. But eventually, they found that they were just going through the motions. The passion they once had had slowly died. The zeal they once knew was replaced with monotony. The extraordinary had become ordinary, and Jesus called them out: "I hold this against you: You have forsaken the love you had at first" (Revelation 2:4).

We all go through times when the fire of God in our life feels more like a flicker. What does it look like to remember our first love and fan that flame in our lives? As I look to God's Word, I see two practical truths laid out for us which can help us return to that love.

Remember

After God calls out the church of Ephesus about how far they've fallen out of love with Him, the next words that come out of His mouth encourage them to *remember*: "Remember how you once loved Me" (Revelation 2:5 NLV). The act of remembering is profoundly healing. I use this idea in counseling on a regular basis. When paired with wisdom and a healthy perspective, our ability to recall, consider, and remember our past can lead us to healing. Part of healing from past trauma requires us to remember and process that trauma. Part of healing from hurts in a relationship requires us to remember the things we love and cherish about the relationship. Remembering helps us see things in proper perspective because it gives us the big picture of who we are and where we've come from. God calls His people to remember the relationship they once had with Him as part of rekindling the flame of their first love. Remember how you were transformed! Remember your excitement! Remember your passion! Remember all that God has done in your life and why you chose to follow Him. Remember God. Remember His love. Remember His grace. Remember His freedom.

Return

Remembering is the first step to healing. But it's not enough to remember if we don't start doing things differently. The second step that God lays out for the church of Ephesus is to repent and return to the way they were once living! "Repent and do the things you did at first!" (Revelation 2:5). In other words, stop doing what you are doing, and start doing the good things you used to do! Just like with other relationships, when we first enter a relationship with Jesus, we usually find ourselves in the season of spring. Our emotions are high, our passion is strong, our commitment is clear. We give all our energy and invest all our time. We pray, read, study, and get involved in everything we possibly can to further our relationship with Him.

But as time goes on, the excitement of spring starts to fizzle. The burdens of life start to weigh down our joy and our passion. We start taking things for granted and forget who really holds all things together. We start relying on ourselves more and more and on Him less and less. Slowly, as our actions cool off, so does our passion.

Maybe you find yourself reading this today, questioning what happened to your first love. I know that is a message that resonates with me. It's easy for my relationship with Jesus to take a back burner to my marriage, my family, my life. It's easy to compartmentalize my connection with Him as a portion of my day, rather than see Him as the very source of my life. It's even easy to allow my work for Jesus to overshadow my love for Jesus. But real relationships don't work that way, and neither should our relationship with Him.

Real-life relationships require time, affection, energy, communication, passion, and commitment. They require me to remember—when I don't feel like remembering. Real-life relationships require repentance, even when I don't want to admit that I have been wrong. They call me to change, to do the things I once did. And when I can begin to see my connection with Jesus as a real-life, living, breathing relationship, it begins to change everything because it begins to change *me*. Remember your first love, and then allow that love to fill you up and begin to overflow into every part of your life and into every other relationship.

Is It Hot in Here?

For John's birthday this year, I signed us up for a glass-blowing class. He's always been fascinated by stained glass and glass sculptures, and it has been a dream of his to learn the process of shaping glass. We pulled up to the oversized garage, and out came our quirky instructor. With his messy hair, protective goggles, and stained clothes, he looked like an artsy mad scientist. But he was brilliant. With comfort and ease, he showed us how a simple flame of fire could take a stem of solid glass and turn it into a soft putty that resembled a liquid more than a solid. But the fire had to be *hot*—2000 degrees Fahrenheit, to be exact. It is hard to comprehend something that hot until you get closer. Even from several feet away, we could feel the immense heat of that little flame blowing waves of hot air onto our bodies. Within moments, sweat was dripping down every single part of our bodies. Talk about a hot date!

We watched closely as he held the stem of glass to the flame because we knew soon it would be our turn to try. He added fragments of color, swirled it around, stretched it, and eventually, he even blew into the stem, causing the liquid glass to form the shape of a large bubble. He put the hot glass bubble back into the fire, and with his special scissors, he slowly started cutting off the top of the bubble to create a beautiful vase sculpture. Little by little, his masterpiece came to life right before our eyes. Yet, with every step, the fire was the key element. "Let the fire do its work," he continually reminded us. As soon as he took the sculpture out of the fire, it would instantly lose its malleability. Without the fire, the glass would remain rigid and immovable. Without the fire, there would be no change, no transformation. Without the fire, there would be no masterpiece.

When it was finally my turn to hold the glass to the hot fire, I couldn't help but think of my own life as that little stem, being molded and transformed by the fire of God. I could choose to come close to that powerful flame and be transformed or keep at a comfortable distance but remain the same. It is an either-or situation. You are either in the fire, or you are not. There is no in-between option. You either choose to get uncomfortably hot, or you don't. Change will never happen at a distance. Scripture calls our God a "consuming fire" (Hebrews 12:29) because it is not possible to get near to Him and stay the same. His fire will always refine us (Zechariah 13:9 esv). His fire will always purify us (Malachi 3:3 esv).

When you consider the power of God's transforming fire at work in your life, you realize how important it is to be in a relationship with someone who is also being shaped by that consuming fire. I don't simply trust my husband to become a better man; I trust God's consuming Spirit at work in his life to mold him, to change him, and to transform him in the way that only God Himself could do. John doesn't simply trust me to be an amazing wife; he trusts God's transforming work in my life to convict me, to purify me, and to refine me. We don't simply trust each other; we trust the fire at work in each other's lives. It is only in the fire that the masterpiece can come to life.

My prayer for you is that you would be compelled to draw near to the consuming fire of God, that His flame would begin to change you, to refine you, and to convict you. I pray that in His fire, your heart would become as soft as putty in His hands. I pray that you would stay close to that fire and allow Him to mold you, to stretch you, and to transform you—and then watch as that transformed heart begins to impact the relationships around you. My prayer for your relationships is that you would find someone who is willing to live life by your side under the consuming fire of God. If you are single, I'm asking God to open your eyes to the importance of His Spirit as a primary ingredient in the health of your future marriage, and that you would cling firmly to that desire. If you are married, I'm asking God to be at work in your life and in the life of your spouse, whether they are near to God or not. May you remain close to Jesus and trust Him to be at work in your life and at work in the life of your spouse in ways that only He can. May each and every single one of us choose to remain close to His consuming fire so that we can be healed, purified, and changed. May the fire of summer burn brightly in each of our lives.

Reflection Questions for Couples

1. Not only is it important to marry someone who is spiritually "on fire," it is just as important to become someone like that. What is your current spiritual temperature? How are you cultivating "the fire of the Spirit of God" in your personal life?

2. In what ways is your spiritual temperature (whether cold or hot) impacting your marriage? What are some steps you can take as a couple to fan the flame of God's Spirit in your relationship?

3. Is there anything in your personal life that God wants to refine and correct? How are you allowing His Spirit to bring these things to your attention?

Reflection Questions for Singles

1. Not only is it important to look for someone who is spiritually "on fire," it is just as important to become someone like that. What is your current spiritual temperature? How are you cultivating "the fire of the Spirit of God" in your personal life?

2. How do you react to the suggestion of not praying together early on in a dating relationship? Have you ever experienced the negative effects of a lack of spiritual boundaries in a relationship?

3. Is there anything in your personal life that God wants to refine and correct? How are you allowing His Spirit to bring these things to your attention?

FALL—YOUR TRUE COLORS

Fall is the season when the green starts to fade and your true colors begin to shine. In fall, you realize that you are two very different people with unique personalities, ideas, and interests.

Not only do your true colors begin to shine, but so do the colors of your partner as you start seeing them for who they really are—strengths and weaknesses, flaws and failures, quirks and habits.

In this season, the leaves begin to fall as the bare branches are exposed, and you realize that you've got nowhere left to hide. It's an invitation toward the beauty of true vulnerability and authenticity as you learn to get comfortable with dropping the cover and revealing your true self.

In fall, your compatibility is tested, and your connection is tried as you figure out how to manage the complex issues of communication and hard topics of conflict. And you either learn to work through the problems, or you get stuck in them. Fall is an invitation to go deeper than you've ever gone before, but only if you're brave enough to accept the challenge.

7

GOODBYE, GREEN—THE COLORS OF COMPATIBILITY

f I could invite you to my house for a cup of morning coffee, I'd invite you in the fall. From the end of September to the beginning of November, my kitchen window looks like a stained-glass masterpiece. The two large trees just behind our house—one with its vibrant orange hues, the other with its golden yellow shimmer—come together in a remarkable way as the bright sun shines through their leaves and right onto my kitchen floor.

For a fall-lover like me, it is the absolutely best scene to behold. One of the first things I do while my coffee is brewing is open the door in my kitchen that leads outside to the deck and let the cool breeze in. And that crisp air of autumn, combined with the colorful fall foliage outside of my window, is one of my favorite things to wake up to in the morning.

When we chose our home, I had no idea this would be one of my favorite things about it. In fact, I don't remember much about seeing our house for the first time at all. When we first moved to this area, we were in a rush to find somewhere to live. We had planned to live with my parents for a few months as my husband settled into his new job and got acquainted to life in a new place. But after a few months, with two kids ages four and under and a baby on the way…it became evident that we needed to find a home and settle into a routine—and fast!

This home came on the market unexpectedly, and since we didn't have any babysitters that day, we decided to haul the kids over to look at it in a last-ditch effort to find ourselves a place to live.

The people who used to live here were rather…grown up. Nothing in the home was "kid friendly." There were porcelain plates on display in every room, antique furniture in every corner, and things that could shatter and break with every turn. John and I found ourselves running through the house as fast as we possibly could to make sure we could see it before one of our kids broke something! It ended up being the house we chose, and the day we moved in almost felt like our first look at it because we had been so rushed the first time through. Thankfully, as we have gotten to know this house of ours over the past few years, we've found many more things that we love about it than not, but it could have gone the other way. When you finally begin to settle in to something, you start seeing it for what it is rather than for what you hope it to be. You start seeing its quirks, blemishes, and flaws. You start seeing the cracks, dents, and stains. You see it authentically. You see it for what it is.

True Colors

If you give anything enough time, its true colors will eventually show up. The same thing applies to relationships. Sometimes, those colors will surprise you; other times, they'll scare you. The season of fall is all about seeing a relationship for what it really is. Fall is about realizing that in addition to the vibrant green leaves of summer, there are other colors pushing to come up to the surface—the true colors of fall. These can be all kinds of colors: colors displaying the browns of selfishness, the greens of envy, the reds of anger. The true colors of fall can be the purples of pride, the blues of sadness, and the grays of fear and doubt. They can be colors that shine bright with the yellows of joy, the pinks of peace, and the whites of loyalty and trust, or colors displaying the golds of integrity and the silvers of wisdom. We've all got true colors that eventually make their way to the surface of who we are, and when we are in a relationship long enough, our true colors will eventually be seen by those around us. The good colors, the bad colors, and the ugly colors.

Many Different Colors

John and I have *a lot* in common. We are both the firstborn children in our families. We are both goal-oriented. We both like watching cheesy Christian movies. We have very similar spending habits and views on money. We share the same beliefs, morals, and values. And we even sort of look alike.

Similarities are usually the first things that bring you together in a relationship. This makes sense because you initially bond and connect based on the things that you have in common. It was a few months into our relationship when we really started noticing our differences.

John's laid back. I'm structured.

He's funny. I'm serious.

He's logical. I'm creative.

He doesn't like his food touching. I like to mix mine all together and then top it off with a couple of sauces.

He's a private person. I'm an open book.

He processes things by thinking about them. I process things by talking about them.

As our relationship progressed, the green leaves of our similarities started to fade, exposing the colors of our differences. Summer was turning into fall. Goodbye, green.

Often, in the beginning of a relationship, you get a glimpse of the differences but see them through a spring filter and think of them as "cute" or "unique." But, in time, you begin to see those cute and unique things through the filter of fall as frustrating, irritating, or annoying. This is why it is so important to take the time to pass through every one of the seasons of a relationship.

The Story of Mike and Monica

Mike and Monica met in college. There was an instant physical attraction in their distinct differences: Mike loved Monica's dark, exotic features, and she was taken with his blond hair and blue eyes. He was the star of the basketball team. She had her nose buried in books. She was dedicated to her faith. He wasn't quite sure what he believed. She was the bubbly extrovert who always had something to say. He was the reserved introvert with the quiet demeanor. Their different colors seemed so obvious to everyone who knew them, but they didn't see it that way. They were only aware of their strong mutual feelings for one another—a passionate connection that they had never experienced before. They were engaged to be married within months.

Fast-forward ten years into their marriage when I met them, and they were struggling with some major concerns. His lack of communication and inability to express his emotions were shutting her out of his life. Her strong personality and incessant need for conversation was wearing him down and causing him to feel suffocated. They couldn't see eye to eye about anything, and with each passing day, their emotional connection was growing further and further apart. It felt like their world was falling apart, but really, they were struggling through the season of fall.

Compatibility

When it comes to relationships, we don't discuss the importance of compatibility often enough. While some might define compatibility to mean similarities in a relationship, I like to see compatibility as the *ability* to *come together*. Compatibility is the ability to work together and to see life from the other person's perspective. It is the ability to find value and worth in what the other person brings to the relationship.

On one hand, similarities in a relationship do make compatibility easier. The more similar you are in your perspective, the easier it is to see life through the other person's eyes. On the other hand, differences can add depth and excitement to a couple's relationship. Differences can be the catalyst toward growth, maturity, and well-roundedness. Yet, at the end of the day, it is not simply the sum of a couple's differences or similarities that makes or breaks them, it's their compatibility—their ability to handle those differences. Compatibility is a couple's ability to come together, respect, learn from, and appreciate each other in their differences. Naturally, the more differences, the more effort, energy, and investment it takes to "come together." The more compatible a couple is—the more they can "come together" in the many aspects of their life—the less stress they'll face in their relationship.

The Colors of Compatibility

In chapter 2, I discussed the importance of finding a partner whose personality type is compatible with yours, but there are many other areas of compatibility that are highlighted in the season of fall.

Communication Style

Some people prefer to talk through things out loud, while others prefer to think through things internally. Without compatibility, it can easily become a game of cat and mouse. "Cats" want to deal with things as soon as they come up; whereas "mice" would rather run and hide and sort through their thoughts first. These differences can create conflict and tension in a relationship. But no matter how you are wired, the underlying key to compatibility is to ask yourself this: Are you both able to see the importance of conversation and communication and work toward that common goal despite your different communication styles?

Emotional Temperament

Have you ever noticed that some people are hard to read emotionally, while others wear their heart on their sleeve? Or maybe you've noticed that some people tend to have a positive view of life, always looking at the bright side, while others have a negative view of life, always seeing the dark side. All of these emotional expressions make up our emotional temperament. Understanding the differences in our emotional temperament is an important part of achieving compatibility in a relationship.

Cultural Background

Cultural norms go way beyond the food we enjoy and the clothing we wear. Cultural norms influence how we see the world. Oftentimes, we don't even recognize the influence of our cultural norms until we step outside of them and experience someone else's cultural norms. For example, some cultures value productivity above all, while other cultures value relationships. Some cultures show respect by being reserved and mild, while other cultures show love by being warm and bold in their interactions.

Thanks to my Egyptian heritage, I come from one of those warm and bold cultures. Walk into any family gathering, and you'll be greeted by very loud voices, receive multiple hugs from people you've never met, and then be handed a plate full of food and told to sit down and eat (that is, if you can find a place to sit, because often it's standing room only)! Growing up, I personally thought these noisy, busy, food-filled gatherings were everyone's norm—until I was invited to my friend's home for a family gathering. Walking into her home, my buffet-style free-for-all meal was replaced by a table that had exactly four plates for four people, and where my loud-voiced relatives were traded for people who smiled at me more than they talked to me. Our cultural norms are so ingrained in us that we don't often recognize them until we step into someone else's world.

If we're not aware, different cultural norms can easily be misinterpreted and misconstrued. To my friend, my culture can seem suffocating and overwhelming. But to me, her culture can seem cold and aloof. Your differences in cultural background will have a big impact on your ability to see eye to eye. Are you both willing to see the world from the other person's vantage point and learn from their point of view, or do you tend to hold on tightly to your own perspective?

Financial Perspective

It's often said that the number-one issue causing stress and tension in marriages revolves around finances.[1] But how you approach and handle money is a *learned* behavior. Some people are spenders, and some are savers. Our family of origin and life experiences have influenced our perspective on money. Not only do differences in financial responsibility add stress to a relationship, so do differences in socioeconomic status. Your socioeconomic status informs a lot of your personal expectations and desires when it comes to material things, so differences in this aspect of life can cause major stress. Financial differences can add tension to a relationship unless both people are willing to come together, work together, and learn from one another.

Age Differences

I get asked a lot of questions about age differences in relationships. For the most part, there isn't much to think about when the age difference is five years or less. And the more mature a person is, the less these differences come into play. Nevertheless, there's no denying that major age differences play a role when it comes to adding stress to a relationship. With an increased age gap come differences in what I like to call "generational culture." What I mean by that is every generation, or demographic cohort, comes with its own set of attitudes, beliefs, interests, knowledge, experiences, and norms. Each group can be so different that they earn their own designations, like Baby Boomers, Gen Xers, Millennials, and Generation Z.

Every ten years of life brings its own set of differences regarding life experiences and struggles. Those who fall within the same age decade tend to have more in common as they experience life together, which results in less marital stress. We live in a culture that praises "robbing the cradle" and dating the "sugar daddy," without taking into consideration the stress that comes with age differences. And adding to that, relationships made up of age differences greater than 15 years likely come with their own set of deep-seated issues or unaddressed needs (power, security, control, etc.). Compatibility means that both parties bring an awareness of the differences that age can present and a willingness to work them out.

Educational Differences

This is probably one of the less frequently addressed compatibility issues on the list. Most people, myself included, hardly consider the differences that come with levels of education. I'm not referring to differences in occupation or educational focus (though that may or may not be a source of stress for some couples), but rather differences within levels of education completed, such as high school, college, or graduate school. Education informs much of who we are, what we like, and how we invest our time. Education can impact things as simple as what we talk about and the hobbies we develop. People who have the same levels of education tend to have more in common, which offers more fuel for connection. Education level should be considered when it comes to the factors that add stress to a relationship, and what is required to work through that tension.

Lifestyle Habits

Some people are messy, while others are tidy. Some would rather go to a movie, while others would rather grab a good book. Some people love waterskiing, while others would prefer jumping waves at the beach. Lifestyle differences impact what we enjoy and how we spend our time. I know a couple who is struggling to achieve compatibility because of their completely different lifestyles. He's an athletic outdoorsman who loves hiking, biking, canoeing, and camping. She's a nonathletic homebody, who loves to snuggle on the couch and read book after book in front of her cozy fireplace. This became an issue in their marriage because of the drastic difference in their needs and desires and their inability to come together and learn from each other. Again, the differences do not make or break a relationship, but how a couple chooses to navigate those differences can. Whether that means finding a mutual hobby or choosing to take turns enjoying each other's hobbies, compatibility and coming together take more time, energy, and effort with each difference that presents itself.

Morals and Values

One of the most important areas of compatibility has to do with a person's beliefs, morals, and values. Your core values determine how you will live your life based on the actions, decisions, and choices you believe to be wrong and right. They also influence what you believe to be right and wrong in the context of your relationship. Morals and values are different from every other area listed above because a person's view of right and wrong is not something that can or should be set aside in a relationship. Compatibility in this area means finding someone with whom you can connect without setting aside your core views and beliefs. For example, if you believe in monogamy and commitment, and they do not, it doesn't matter how wonderful they are in every other area because you are not compatible. Getting to know a person's core values and beliefs is an important part of understanding whether or not someone is going to be a good match for your life.

The Art of a Good Match

There are two kinds of people: those who love puzzles, and those who don't. I fit more in the latter category. All those little pieces, all that time, energy, and investment to put a picture together one tiny piece at a time—only to take it apart again and put it back in the box! Something about that doesn't seem totally sane to me. But, alas, I do puzzles. Why? Because my kids love them.

It is fun to watch my kids learn the art of putting a puzzle together. When they were younger, there was no rhyme or reason to their madness. They would take any two pieces from the pile and try jamming them together until they got lucky. That method not only takes forever, but also ends up with a dozen bent and broken puzzle pieces that were never meant to be together. The art of putting a puzzle together is in learning to recognize the types of pieces that fit together. Proper puzzle technique is about taking two pieces and learning to look at the shape and colors of each piece in order to begin matching them up accordingly. That's not to say the pieces are going to be identical—they never are. But they fit together.

> In order to know if someone is going to
> be a good match for our lives, we've first
> got to understand our own colors.

Healthy relationships also require us to understand the art of a good match and the importance of compatibility. They require two people who are willing and ready to get to know their colors in order to understand whether or not they'll be a good match—whether or not they'll fit together. But in order to know if someone is going to be a good match for our lives, we've first got to understand our own colors. We have to know our temperament, communication style, and lifestyle preferences. We have to dig deep into our values, morals, and beliefs. We must have a good understanding of who we are, where we've come from, and where we are going in order to see if the person we are with can come along for the ride. Finding a good match for your life starts with recognizing the type of person who fits into your story.

If you are single and reading these pages today, I want you to hear me: Beware of acting from desperation, grabbing a piece from the pile of relationships and frantically jamming it in, trying to make it fit. You may feel tired, lonely, and like time is running out. *If I can't find something that fits, I'm just going to make it fit,* you may be telling yourself. You might try and try to make that relationship work, even though you and your significant other are totally incompatible. If you go that route, you end up with a broken heart—bent and bruised from a lack of discernment and understanding. But this doesn't have to be the process because the more you know yourself, the better you'll recognize the type of person who matches your life.

For those of us who are married, it is important for us to acknowledge that our differences don't have to destroy us if we come at them in a healthy way. Compatibility is not something we find; it is something we must choose. It is something we must pursue. The first step to moving toward compatibility is really *seeing* and *appreciating* our differences rather than simply *looking through* them. Sometimes, we get so accustomed to how things are that we react instead of stepping back to ask the important questions. Why do we come to the table with different perspectives? What has shaped our temperaments and communication styles? Where is there room for growth and change and healing? How are we going to choose to come together? Piece by piece, little by little, question by question, we can start seeing the big picture of this relationship, working together to create something beautiful and filled with all kinds of magnificent colors.

Goodbye, green. It's time for something a little more colorful.

Reflection Questions for Couples

1. As a couple, make a list of your similarities, and then make a list of your differences.

2. Are there any differences that have become frustrating or tend to cause tension and conflict in your relationship? How so?

3. Read through the list of "compatibility" issues that tend to come up in a relationship. Which areas tend to be problem spots in your relationship? How can you allow these differences to add to your relationship rather than to take away from it?

Reflection Questions for Singles

1. Read through the list of compatibility issues that tend to come up in a relationship. Which compatibility issues have impacted you in past relationships or friendships?

2. Which compatibility issues have you seen come up in the lives of other couples you know or in your family of origin?

3. Finding a good match for your life starts with recognizing the type of person who fits into your story. What are you doing to develop insight and awareness of who you are and what you need in a relationship? List three things you can do this month to pursue self-awareness.

8

VIBRANT COLORS—
CONFLICT IS KEY

Have you thought about how amazing your TV is lately? My guess is, probably not, because TVs have become such a normal part of our everyday experience. We get so accustomed to what we have in front of us that it becomes the norm. I grew up in the '80s and '90s, when TVs were big, bulky, and sometimes so pixelated that you could barely make out the details of someone's face. Now, we have flat screens, smart screens, and everything is in high definition. The colors are bold, bright, and beautiful. You can see every fleck in someone's eye, every drop of sweat coming down their face, every wrinkle and crease. Every color, every curve, every shape assaults the eye with information. Thanks to modern technology, you can see every detail on an image—far above and beyond what your naked eye can see.

In a way, relationships also work like that—especially our closest relationships. From a distance, relationships always look tame because you cannot see all the details. Everything sort of blends together, and it all looks decent. But with time, commitment, and intimacy—all of a sudden, things move into high definition. You start seeing all the nitty-gritty details—bright and bold. All the colors that once presented in muted colors and faded hues are now glaring at you in neon.

The girlfriend who struggled with being on time is now the wife who's killing you with her constant tardiness.

The introverted husband whose sweetness captured your heart is now the husband who never opens up.

With time, with the passing of fall, the colors turn vibrant as the season of our relationship begins to change.

Seeing in HD

I don't know exactly when I started really experiencing this with John. Probably somewhere around the two-year mark, our differences went from muted colors to bright and bold. I started seeing him in HD. Every flaw, every imperfection, everything he was missing and everything I wanted him to change were clearer to me than they had ever been.

One thing you should know about me is that I'm one of those people who is heavier on the justice than the mercy. I like things to be at their best. I want wrongs to be made right. I want to find the problem and deal with it. This is part of what draws me to counseling. But it is also the reason John and I get into our most common dance of conflict. I say dance because conflict involves two people. You can't have conflict if only one person is engaging (or disengaging). It takes two to tango, and every couple has their go-to dance, their pattern of relating and interacting. Their theme of give-and-take. Their primary source of conflict—a conflict that comes up time, and time, and time again. Every couple has one (sometimes more than one). Ours usually goes something like this:

Typically, it starts with me noticing something about him that's bothering me. It might be his tone. It could be his time management. It may even be his "laid-backness." But whatever it is, something that was once a muted color all of a sudden turns bright and bold. I see it in high definition, and it starts driving me crazy. So, naturally, I bring it up.

I tell him all about this *thing* that's bothering me, why I think he needs to change it, and how it is impacting our relationship. I'm usually calm, conversational, and clear. I am a counselor, after all. But, instead of receiving my heartfelt criticism with open arms, usually he gets defensive, tells me I'm overreacting, and explains why it is not that big of a deal. And instead of trying to see his point, listening without reservation, and toning it down, I usually get more worked up, see bright and bold and even neon colors all over the place, and overreact. And on and on the dance goes, until one of us is ready to stop seeing in HD and bring it back to real life.

Seeing Too Much

With all the modern technology and advancement of the computer age, we have gotten better at "seeing" with our devices than we can see with our actual human eyes. My husband bought a camera that he could point to the sky and see details on the moon that he could never see with his naked eye. With a simple device, we can see overwhelming detail from thousands of miles away.

There is a reason our eyes don't naturally see with that level of vision on a regular basis. We are not made to see in that type of resolution because it would be too much for our brains to process day in and day out. Our brains would constantly be in overdrive until something would eventually give out or break down. Sometimes, seeing too much can be just as harmful as not seeing enough.

When it comes to healthy relationships, it is important for us to recognize when we are "seeing too little" (avoiding conflict, ignoring issues, being passive, holding back our needs), but it is just as important to note when we are "seeing too much" (being overly critical, blowing things out of proportion, being judgmental, always focusing on the negative and not the positive). In the season of fall, we have the tendency to see things even more vividly than we normally do.

Not only do we see things brightly in fall, but we can also feel things more boldly too. The people you care about the most tend to solicit the strongest feelings from you. Sometimes, these are such strong feelings that they even surprise you. Have you ever noticed that someone can say something slightly negative to you, and it doesn't bother you that much, but if your spouse or boyfriend or girlfriend makes that same comment to you, the volcano of emotions erupts? People who are closest to us bring out the boldest feelings inside of us. And the dance of conflict goes on.

The Dance of Conflict

According to relationship expert and researcher Dr. John Gottman, 69 percent of problems in a relationship are what he calls "unsolvable."[1] What he means by that is that at the end of the day, much of the conflict that comes up in our relationships is based on differences in perspectives, personality, or deep-seated beliefs. They are things that won't just magically go away. They are things that are not *easily* going to change. For example:

- Jen is laid back with time and is late to everything, but Mike sees time as money and values being punctual.

- Andrew is an extrovert who wants to socialize every chance he gets, but Melissa is an introvert who needs her alone time to recharge.

- Rebecca appreciates organization and structure in her living environment, but Seth doesn't feel the same and prefers his space to be a creative mess.

- Josh feels things deeply and makes his decisions based on what he feels in his heart, but Erin is a thinker and wants to process every detail logically before a decision is made.

These are the types of conflict-inducing differences in a relationship that Gottman would see as "unsolvable," which means that rather than try to fix them, we have to learn how to cope with them. Bring any two people together, and you are going to find a long list of conflict-inducing problems. It does not matter if you marry Julie or Andrea. It doesn't matter if you marry Brian or Chris. Maybe you end up with someone who's not always late, but they are really messy. Or maybe you find yourself married to someone who is great with a budget but terrible at expressing their emotions. Everyone comes with their personal baggage of issues that you'll eventually start to unpack and begin the process of learning how to cope. In fact, Dr. Gottman goes as far as to say, "Marriages are successful to the degree that the problems you choose are ones you can cope with."[2] The bottom line is this: You are going to have a different set of conflicts with each combination of people, so make sure it is a set you can live with.

You are going to have a different set of
conflicts with each combination of people,
so make sure it is a set you can live with.

Coping Versus Character

With this in mind, let me clarify that there is a huge difference between the average conflict that we learn to cope with in a relationship and major character flaws. When we are talking about dealing with conflict with someone who is late versus someone who is on time, or differing views about how we should handle the in-laws, or different perspectives on the budget—we are *not* referring to major character flaws that come up in a relationship. When it comes to character issues like deceit or dishonesty, pornography or sexual promiscuity, unhealthy behaviors or addictions, inappropriate relationships with the opposite sex or a lack of boundaries, anger outbursts or rage, violence or abuse, etc., we need to see these issues in a different light. We're not meant to simply learn to "cope" with these types of issues; we're meant to call them out and demand change.

I *expect* my husband to take responsibility for his heart and mind by staying away from pornography and lustful thoughts. But I don't expect him to change his personality to be more of an extrovert when he's not wired that way.

He *expects* me to bring total honesty with everything I'm doing, where I'm going, and with whom I'm interacting. But he doesn't expect me to stop being structured and organized when I'm wired that way.

Some conflicts are a matter of coping that we need to learn to work through; others are a matter of character where we need to expect change—and we need to get really good at recognizing the difference and seeking professional help when we're not sure which is which.

For a list of conflicts a couple can work through, refer to the previous chapter regarding compatibility issues such as communication styles, emotional temperament, cultural background, financial perspective, age differences, educational differences, lifestyle habits, and morals and values.

Connecting Versus Correcting

One of the best ways to deal with conflict is to start seeing it as an opportunity. I recently interviewed conflict expert and psychologist Dr. Les Parrott on my *Love + Relationships* podcast, where he said, "Conflict is the price we pay for a deeper level of intimacy." What a beautiful way to look at conflict. We tend to believe that conflict is bad and should be avoided at all costs, but that view is neither accurate nor healthy.

Conflict is an opportunity. It is the key we hold in our hand that invites us to connect in a way we never could have otherwise. If we see conflict that way, rather than avoid it, we can learn to use it as an opportunity to draw closer to one another. Conflict is about more than simply correcting behaviors and finding ways to cope with an issue; it is about learning to connect.

Making the Most of Conflict

Now that we have a better framework for understanding conflict, we have to practice using conflict to bring us closer together rather than to push us apart. If you are married and you are dealing with conflict right now in the season of fall, I encourage you to really take these next steps to heart. Study them, memorize them, and begin applying them to how you deal with conflict. If you are dating or single, start by learning how to apply these principles to the conflict in your personal life, and then make sure you expect the same level of healthy conflict management in the person you date.

#1: Prepare for It

I despise car trouble. It brings back traumatic memories of being a college student with a "beater" car and getting stranded on the road at least a dozen times a year. I remember one winter morning when I went to get in my car to drive to a midterm exam. After unlocking my car door, as I went to take my key out of the door's lock, the entire door lock *came out on my key*! Then, for some odd reason, all the automatic windows rolled down, and the car alarm started blaring.

When you are a broke college student, having a lemon for a car is truly a burden because car trouble equals money trouble. When you have no money in the bank, figuring out how to fix the problem is another problem in and of itself.

Conflict in relationships works the same way. You have to have emotional and relational "money in the bank" in order to prepare for the problems that will inevitably come up. If your emotional tank is always empty, when problems arise, you are going to find yourself unable to deal with those problems. If you think of conflict as the problems that withdraw "money" from your emotional account, you have to prepare for conflict by having positive emotional connections before conflict comes up. Your reservoir has to be filled in order for you to be able to tackle problems as they come.

> You have to prepare for conflict by having positive emotional connections before conflict comes up. Your reservoir has to be filled in order for you to be able to tackle problems as they come.

This involves thinking ahead and being deliberate to "fill up the account" of your relationship. Here are some simple suggestions:

- Make time to connect with a few minutes of meaningful conversation each day.

- Ask each other questions and make it a point to be interested and attentive to the answers.

- Be deliberate about finding one way to serve your loved one each day.

- Use physical touch (holding hands, unexpected kisses, an arm around a shoulder, a hand on the back as you are passing by) on a regular basis to show affection and love.

- Find time frequently to get away to focus on your connection.

- Take part in fun activities that build your friendship and emotional connection.

- Go over the top with words of encouragement throughout the day.

- Send text messages, write notes, and take the time to express your affection through written words.

- Buy a thoughtful gift (it doesn't have to be expensive) to show your appreciation and love.

When your emotional account is filled up, you'll be prepared and able to withdraw from your account by dealing with conflict as it arises.

#2: Don't Fear Conflict

Some people believe that the best way to deal with conflict is to avoid it altogether. Maybe they are people pleasers and would rather stay quiet than upset someone. Maybe they don't have the energy for a controversial interaction. Maybe they struggle with expressing themselves, so they just stay quiet instead. Whatever the case, some people really believe that it is better to flee from a problem than to face it. But those people are wrong. Passivity in a relationship may avoid conflict for a little while, but it just ends up piling up under the rug. And eventually, that pile gets so high that someone ends up tripping over it.

If conflict is really the road to deepened intimacy, then dealing with conflict head-on must be part of the equation of a healthy relationship. You can't be afraid of it. If you are in a relationship in which there is little to no conflict, that tells me someone is holding something back. Once you've taken the time to build up your emotional account and prepare for conflict, you have nothing to fear going into it. Shifting your perspective on conflict is an important part of handling conflict well.

#3: Know Your Style

An important part of dealing with conflict is understanding your approach to conflict. When you understand your conflict style, you'll be able to see the pros and cons of your style and make changes that will benefit your relationship. Generally speaking, there are five types of people when it comes to conflict styles.[3]

Avoiders would prefer not to deal with the issue rather than face it. Avoidance can prove to be beneficial regarding a situation that has nothing to do with you. But, for the most part, avoiding conflict in your personal relationships ends up causing more harm in the long run because it creates an environment ripe for bitterness and contempt.

Accommodators are less passive than avoiders. They might engage in the conflict, but they end up sacrificing themselves in the conflict rather than trying to find a middle ground. They would much rather be the one to give up something than ask others to do so. They're very cooperative but often end up in situations in which they are struggling or feeling bitterness because they are not willing or able to say what they need.

Compromising people know what they want, but they are willing to meet in the middle. They want to find a solution that works for everyone, including themselves! They're willing to give a little to get a little and expect the same of others. They're okay with the idea of 50-50, and seek to resolve situations with that philosophy in mind.

Collaborative people want to find a solution in which "everyone wins." They are highly assertive, know what they want, and are quick to express their desires. Instead of "giving a little to get a little," they would rather keep working together to find a solution that works for everyone.

Competitive people tend to be assertive and at times even aggressive. They know what they want and often see it as "my way or the highway." They are firm in their beliefs and have a hard time giving up or walking away from what they want. Sometimes, in their desire to get what they want, they can end up ruining relationships or hurting feelings because of their tendency to see their viewpoint to the exclusion of seeing from the perspective of others.

There are limitations and benefits to each of these conflict styles. But knowing your conflict style is important because it allows you to see the strengths and weaknesses in how you approach problems and alter your style accordingly.

#4: Understand Before Being Understood

A while back we attended a party at our friends' house, where we got to meet their sweet 90-something grandma. At one point in the evening, Grandma was walking toward me with her cane in hand, when her son started calling her name from across the room. She kept walking toward me without looking to the left or the right, as if she didn't hear a thing, which is to be expected when you are 90-something years old. But, as she slowly moved closer to me, this feisty old woman looked me straight in the eye, gave me a smiling wink, and said, "They think I'm too old to hear them, so I might as well use it to my advantage." I couldn't believe my ears! I almost died from laughing so hard.

No matter what your conflict style, and no matter how old or young you are, at the end of the day, the key to being successful in your relationships really comes down to your listening skills—and whether or not you choose to use them. Listening is the chief component of good communication. That means you cannot be an effective communicator and you cannot possibly be good at managing conflict if you aren't a good listener. That might be hard news for some of us to swallow, especially those of us who like to talk more than we like to listen.

In addition to the communication benefits of listening, God's Word is crystal clear: It is better to be quick to listen and slow to speak (James 1:19). Most of us go into conflict ready to say what we need, express our opinions, and give our side of the story. But the most effective communication happens when we can take a step back and make it our priority to understand before being understood. Oftentimes, when we understand first, the problem solves itself! Sometimes all it takes for conflict to blow over is for someone to listen well.

> Sometimes all it takes for conflict to blow
> over is for someone to listen well.

I've found this to be true in my own life and marriage. In the heat of the moment, oftentimes, just feeling like John is listening—really listening—takes down my defenses and helps calm the situation. There have even been times in our marriage where we didn't reach a clear resolution, and we still had different perspectives on the situation in the end, but our ability to listen to one another disarmed the entire conflict and left us feeling more connected than when we started. It's important to take inventory of your listening skills and ask yourself if you approach conflict with the goal of being understood, or the goal of understanding.

#5: Empathize

There's this awful stereotype that we counselors sit around in an office all day long, asking, "How does that make you feel?" to people lying on couches getting therapy. First of all, except for Freudian diehards, I don't know of any counselor who has their clients lie on a couch. Second of all, although acknowledging feelings is important—more than asking, "How does that make you feel?"—what we really try to do in a counseling session is to offer empathy. Empathy is the key to connecting with another human being. It is the opportunity to see life through someone else's eyes, and it is truly life changing.

One of my favorite books about the therapy process is called *The Gift of Therapy* by Irvin Yalom. In this book, Dr. Yalom shares a story about a young woman he was counseling who was struggling with a broken relationship with her negative, "naysaying" father. The last straw in the relationship was when her father drove her down to her college one day. She was hoping for a positive interaction that day, a time of reconciliation as they enjoyed the beautiful scenery of the drive together. Instead, all her father did the entire way was complain about the garbage-littered creek by the side of the road. The creek looked perfectly fine to her, and his bad attitude caused her to shut down and remain silent the rest of the trip, which caused a greater wedge in their relationship. Yalom goes on to tell the rest of the story: "Later, she made that same trip alone and was astounded to see that there were two streams—one on each side of the road. 'This time I was the driver,' she said sadly, 'and the stream I saw through my window on the driver's side was just as ugly and polluted as my father had described it.' But by the time she had learned to look out her father's window, it was too late—her father was dead and buried."[4]

What a sobering reminder of the importance of learning to "look out the other person's window" as the key to what it means to have empathy and understanding in our relationships. Empathy is what brings us into the world of the other and brings perspective and understanding that can restore even the most broken relationships. Don't ever attempt to engage in conflict without it.

#6: Set Boundaries

Any good fight has to come with rules of engagement, boundaries that keep people safe and secure in conflict. Early on in our marriage, my husband and I learned of our tendency to want to walk away when we get upset and leave a conflict unresolved. So, we came up with some "rules of engagement." These rules revolve around keeping us engaged and present even when we don't really want to be: 1) Never walk out on the other person, 2) Never leave in the middle of an argument, and 3) Always seek a resolution before moving on to the next thing.[5] The boundaries and limits we set for ourselves remind us that we are on the same team, working toward a solution together.

Each couple has to identify their tendencies to handle conflict in a negative way and then set boundaries and limits for themselves that prevent them from defaulting to those negative tendencies. If you are a yeller, make it a point to set a boundary for yourself that you will not raise your voice in the middle of a conflict. If you are an avoider, set the boundary that you will not allow yourself to isolate and distract yourself during a conflict, but that you'll face it head-on. If you tend to shut people out, set a boundary that you won't default to your "silent treatment," but instead, will express what you need and what's going on inside of you. Talking through your boundaries and limits *before* conflict comes up is the best way to prepare yourself to handle conflict well *after* it comes up.

#7: Get to the Root

What is really going on here? I tend to ask myself that question on a regular basis in the middle of conflict. So many times, conflict is not actually about the situation that is happening in the here and now. It's about something much deeper—feelings and emotions buried underneath the surface. Our ability to recognize that simple truth will save us much heartache and endless arguments.

Is this really about the fact that he was 20 minutes late, or is it more that I am feeling unimportant and that I'm not a priority?

Is this really about the fact that I need her to pick up this mess, or am I feeling overworked and underappreciated?

Is this really about him correcting me in front of the kids, or am I struggling with insecurity and feeling that I'm not good enough?

Is this really about her not calling me today, or am I feeling unloved and unwanted?

This is often not rooted in *this* at all—but in something else. There are so many feelings, emotions, needs, and deep-seated beliefs underneath the surface of conflict that, if we dig deep, we often find that there are roots to this issue that we haven't really expressed or addressed. We often address the surface reaction, the superficial irritation, or the visible annoyance without actually dealing with the real problem underneath. *What is this really about? How am I really feeling? Why am I reacting in this way? Have I really expressed what's going on inside of me? Have I really asked for deeper needs to be met?* These are the types of questions we need to be asking as we engage in healthy conflict.

This is often not rooted in *this* at all—but in something else.

Sometimes, the answer really is superficial: Yes, I really just need you to help me with these dishes. But other times—oftentimes—we'll find that there's much more going on underneath that we've failed to identify or express. Learning to identify and express those deep feelings and needs is one of the greatest keys to both managing conflict and inviting intimacy.

If conflict is truly the key to deeper intimacy, then I say, "Bring on the conflict!" Because the season of fall, with its bold and bright colors, can truly be a wonderful time of year.

Reflection Questions for Couples

1. Are there any deficiencies or traits in your partner that you tend to see "in high definition"?

2. How do you react to the concept that 69 percent of relationship problems are unsolvable? What type of unsolvable issues have you faced in your relationship? How have you learned to cope and deal with those situations?

3. Conflict is the key to greater intimacy. Read through the list of ways to leverage conflict, and talk through which aspects you could work on together as a couple.

4. With which of the conflict styles listed do you most connect and why?

Reflection Questions for Singles

1. What is your reaction to this statement: "You are going to have a different set of conflicts with each combination of people, so make sure it is a set you can live with." Do you agree or disagree? Why or why not? How does this principle impact the kind of people you choose to date?

2. Conflict is the key to greater intimacy. Read through the list of ways to leverage conflict, and ask yourself which aspects of leveraging conflict you can begin applying to your personal relationships with family and friends.

3. With which of the conflict styles listed do you most connect and why?

9

BARE BRANCHES–
DROPPING THE COVER

or many reasons, it is hard for me to say goodbye to fall. Yet, as I
write this chapter, that is exactly what is happening as November
ticks down, one day at a time.

I hate knowing that this is the last I'll see of the beautiful leaves until
next year. As I look out my window, the gorgeous, vibrant colors of red,
yellow, and orange are quickly starting to drop to the ground, leaving
nothing but the bare branches. Trees look so much worse when their
covering is gone.

But then again, don't we all?

Dropping the Cover

There's a level of safety in covering. For trees, their thick leaves pro-
vide a covering that blankets the branches, protects them from the elements, and gives them a glorious appearance as they sway in the breeze.

We all have an element of covering in our lives, something we use to
protect us and give us the appearance of what we want to be (whether
or not it is true). It could be the makeup that accentuates our features
and covers up blemishes and imperfections. It could be clothing that
highlights our favorite body parts and covers up the not-so-favorites.
It could be our social media profiles that spotlight the things we want
the world to know about us and filter out the things we don't want

them to know. It could be our conversations—our ability to talk up our strengths and minimize our weaknesses. There are so many things we use as coverings in our lives, but once the cover has been dropped, we are faced with nothing but the bare branches.

I wonder what it must have felt like for Adam and Eve to experience that feeling for the first time when their "covering" of innocence was removed? In Genesis chapter 3, we read one of the most significant stories in history introducing us to the very first instance of human depravity and God's glorious plan for redemption and grace. God created a beautiful garden for Adam and Eve and trusted them to care for it. But He warned them to stay away from one particular tree, saying, "You are free to eat from any tree in the garden; but you must not eat from the tree of the knowledge of good and evil, for when you eat from it you will certainly die" (Genesis 2:16-17). But, as we all know, the serpent came and deceived them. They decided to go against God's command and eat from the tree.

Immediately after their sin came the realization of their weakness and vulnerability: "Then the eyes of both of them were opened, and they realized they were naked; so they sewed fig leaves together and made coverings for themselves" (Genesis 3:7). Their covering of innocence had been taken away, and they realized that there was nothing left but the bare branches. They had to find something to hide the dark truth of who they were and what they had done. So, Scripture tells us, they sewed together some leaves and went to hide from God. But I wonder if they were also trying to hide from themselves.

God came and found them in the garden that day and called them out of their sin and disobedience. And in His grace and mercy, He clothed them with a new covering made of garments of skin and sent them off in the world, anticipating the ultimate covering He would soon send to cover the sins of all the world: the precious covering of the blood of His Son, Jesus Christ.

Lies, Lies, Lies

As was the case for Adam and Eve, our coming to terms with reality is one of the most important components of healing and change. There comes a point in each of our lives when we have to learn to "drop the cover" and expose the bare branches of our sins and struggles in order for us to begin to heal. We have to open our eyes to who we really are and make the choice to stop hiding. Oftentimes, it is much easier to hide than it is to be exposed. It is much easier to put on a facade and live with our makeshift covering of fig leaves than it is to come to terms with who we are. It's so much easier to live with lies than to face the truth, especially in a world where we want so desperately to be loved and so much to be liked.

We long for acceptance and belonging to the point where we'll do anything to receive it, even if that means pretending to be something we are not. Scroll through any social media app, look through any dating profile, or turn on any "reality" TV show, and you'll see evidence of that facade right before your eyes—picture-perfect photos, airbrushed faces. We live in a world that is clothed in a makeshift covering. We cover up who we really are in exchange for who we want to be or who we wish we were.

We're so desperate to be wanted that we would rather lie than risk not being liked. A study from the University of Massachusetts found that 60 percent of people were caught lying in a ten-minute conversation when driven by the desire to appear likeable.[1] Participants of the study were unknowingly recorded having a ten-minute conversation, and then had the conversation played back to them in order to identify how many times they lied. Most people didn't lie just once. The participants of this study were caught lying an average of three times in the short conversation, with the higher number of lies ranging up to 12. People who were trying to be perceived as "likeable" tended to tell more outright lies and exaggerations about themselves, as well as lie about their feelings. There was no difference noted between the amount of lies between genders. Men and women lied the same amount—they just lied about different things.

If people tend to lie that often in a random conversational setting, it makes me wonder how much harder it is to be honest in a world in which we are wired to present our best selves. How honest are we with others? How honest are we with God? How honest are we with ourselves? Are there any areas in our life where we need to drop the cover?

Bare Branches

In every relationship, there comes a point when we must choose to drop our cover and expose our true self, asking ourselves whether or not we trust our partner enough to let them in. Sometimes, we hold on to our cover because it protects us. Other times, we hold on to our cover because we are trying to be what everyone else wants us to be, instead of coming to terms with who we are and admitting our flaws and failures.

> In every relationship, there comes a point when we must choose to drop our cover and expose our true self, asking ourselves whether or not we trust our partner enough to let them in.

Honesty is the most important part of building trust in a relationship, and the levels of honesty and authenticity that we must display get more and more significant as the relationship progresses. In the beginning of a relationship, you display a basic level of honesty. You talk through your likes and dislikes, you get to know facts about one another, and you explore each other's personality and interests. But as the relationship progresses, being honest requires a much deeper level of vulnerability. You start sharing your opinions and ideas. You talk through your goals, and dreams, and desires. You learn to be honest about how you think and feel. You start opening up about what you need and what's bothering you. You get real about your weaknesses and failures, your sins and struggles, your past and your mistakes. It can be hard to reach this level of "realness" in our relationships because it is not something that naturally comes with time—it's something we have to be deliberate about achieving and maintaining.

In our culture, we tend to differentiate between big lies and little lies. Maybe it's not okay to lie about with whom you are texting, but it's okay to lie about how you really feel about something. We tend to make exceptions between blatant lies and lies of omission. Maybe it's not okay to lie about where you've been, but it is deemed okay *not to bring it up* if it doesn't come up in conversation. This belief, which minimizes the importance of full disclosure and true authenticity, causes irreversible damage in many relationships.

Building trust in a relationship is like connecting links to make a chain. Each truth is a link that adds another piece to the chain of trust and intimacy between two people. But if you remove a link through dishonesty, it does not matter how big or how little the link is, and it does not matter if you take one link or one hundred—you'll break the chain. You will sever the trust. You will have a broken structure that needs to be repaired.

Hillary and Tom

Hillary and Tom had been dating for over a year, but they were quite far from the prospect of getting married. They met at church through serving on the worship team, and their relationship blossomed right from the beginning. Their dating relationship quickly progressed, and talk of marriage was soon part of the conversation. But things were not as they seemed. About six months into their relationship, Hillary started wondering if Tom was hiding something. He would cancel plans at the last minute or make excuses as to why he couldn't do something. Hillary started noticing that things in his stories didn't always add up. The facts and details of where he was and with whom he was spending time didn't always align. He wasn't open about his interactions with others and got defensive when Hillary would ask him about his text messages or online interactions. Even though Hillary was wired to see the best in people, she started noticing behaviors that she couldn't overlook, and finally decided to ask Tom straight up if he was cheating on her. To her dismay, he was. He broke down and admitted to having a romantic interest in another woman with whom he had shared a kiss. His lies had finally caught up to him, and there was nowhere left to run but toward the truth. Tom was repentant and owned up to his sins and struggles, which included a list of other things of which Hillary wasn't aware—including his struggle with pornography and some deep insecurities.

When Hillary and Tom shared their story with me, they were six months into healing, on the uphill climb of rebuilding trust and restoring their relationship. They were surrounded by supportive friends, enrolled in professional counseling, and determined to get to the root of what had caused Tom's behavior. But they couldn't move forward toward marriage unless the chain of trust was restored and repaired and until there were signs of long-term healing and restoration. It is much easier to build trust in a relationship than it is to repair it after it has been broken. Even with over a year of dating under their belt, they had to start from square one, realizing there were so many things they had "assumed" about one another and never took the time to address in their relationship before.

Don't Assume, Ask

As Christians, we tend to assume the best in people—which is a good thing…until it's not.

We assume that everyone is trustworthy, and we're all doing our best. We assume there are no major issues or underlying sins. We assume that we have our past baggage under control and that we're entering relationships light and free. We assume that there are no red flags or concerns if we don't see them right off the bat. We assume that just because we are Christians, we are going to be good at relationships.

We assume much more often than we ask. But assumption leads us down a path that leaves problems unaddressed rather than dealt with head-on. Over the years as a professional counselor, I have learned that what people look like from the outside is not necessarily who they are on the inside. Take, for instance, the sweet, silver-haired, 80-something-year-old grandma who walked into my counseling practice one day because she was court-ordered to come to counseling after embezzling over $100,000 from the company where she had worked for 25 years. Even little old ladies can hide behind their covering. I'm not saying that we shouldn't trust anyone, but I am advocating that we don't trust until trust has been earned. Trust is not something you give; it is something that has to be earned. Trust shouldn't be a default reaction—it's a product of intentionality. The building of trust requires time, energy, communication, and a deliberate pursuit of truth.

> Trust is not something you give; it is something that has to be earned.

In order for us to have a healthy perspective and to build trust in a relationship, we have to get better at asking than we are at assuming. We have to be able to have direct, candid, point-blank conversations addressing where we are, as well as where the other person is, in our emotional, spiritual, and psychological health.

Ten Things to Ask, Not Assume

It does not matter if you are looking ahead at marriage or if you have been married 50 years—in order to get through the season of fall, you have to get comfortable with asking rather than assuming. Whether you are in a dating relationship or whether you are currently married, let me walk you through some talking points that you can use as a guide to making sure you are actively pursuing complete honesty and openness in your relationship.

Past

It is crucial to talk about your past because the past has a significant role in shaping the present. Whether your past is tainted with pain or filled with hope, you need to get real about where you come from. Past relationships, family history, and significant experiences (both positive and negative) that have shaped you are just some of the things that need to be discussed as you look back—so that you can join together in moving forward.

Family

What role does your family play in your life, and how does that impact your relationship? How has your family of origin shaped your view of relationships, marriage, love, and communication? How have they shaped your view of self and of God? So much of what you learn about God and about love comes from what you were taught about love as well as how love was modeled to you growing up. It's important to be aware of these things and learn to talk through them with your significant other.

How will visits, holidays, and special occasions impact your relationship with one another? Will you start your own traditions or continue those of your family of origin? What role will your extended family play when it comes to life and decision making? Couples don't often consider the seriousness of combining two separate families. But the joining of families is a process that can cause much strain and stress if it is assumed and not addressed.

Sex

Our views of sex and sexuality are shaped long before we commit to marriage. I know that has been true in my own life. In *Choosing Marriage,* I start the chapter on sex by writing about our completely unrealistic views of honeymoon sex and how those views played out in the most hilarious and awkward way when my husband and I made it back to the honeymoon suite. But let me spare you the details and just give you the kicker of our honeymoon story: Sex didn't happen that night! Not even close. After a few failed attempts, we ended the evening eating wedding-day leftovers and laughing about how Hollywood chick flicks should never be trusted to give you a perspective on real sex. Looking back, I realize how much we needed to learn about, understand, and talk through when it came to sex.

It is crucial to get comfortable with this topic of conversation because it is one that you'll carry on for the rest of your married life. What are your views of sex, and how have they been shaped? What is your past sexual history, and how might that impact your relationship? What expectations do you have, and are you on the same page? Understanding your sexual views and knowing your partner's is a valuable part of preparing for intimacy. It is a conversation that starts before marriage and lasts every step of the way. In marriage, you have to get really good at dropping the cover, exposing what you need in your sexual relationship, and examining how you are wired. Men and women are completely different sexual beings, and a man's sexual "on button" looks completely different than a woman's sexual "on button." If you lead with your assumptions, as couples often do, you are going to end up hurt, frustrated, and disappointed.

Secrets

I get a lot of questions from people wondering when the right time is to share "secrets"—the parts of your life that you rarely share with others, the skeletons in your closet. There is no better time to share these intimate things than when, like Hillary and Tom in the story above, you are looking ahead at marriage. As soon as marriage is part of the equation, it is time to expose the bare branches and let your partner in. From family secrets to personal choices, from health problems to mental health concerns, this is the time to share things big and small, paving the way for honesty and openness as the foundation of your relationship.

I remember vividly the first time I shared a big secret with John. We had been dating for a significant amount of time, and I knew that engagement was right around the corner because we had discussed marriage. One evening, we were sitting together dreaming of our future, when I realized I could not move forward until he knew something. Just before we had started dating, I had been diagnosed with a condition that would likely make it difficult, and maybe even impossible, to have children. At this point in our relationship, the conversation about children had not even come up yet, but I knew I needed to talk with him about my diagnosis.

I will never forget his reaction because it pretty much sealed the deal in my mind that this was the guy I wanted to do life with forever. After I shared my heart, he grabbed my tear-soaked cheeks, looked me straight in the eyes, and without a hint of hesitation, he assured me that whatever problems or issues we faced in the future, we would face them together. He would be right there by my side, walking through the challenges of life, loving me through them. He has upheld that promise in so many ways. My bare branches have been exposed again and again over the past decade of marriage, in ways I could never share in the pages of this book, yet he has loved me so well. Thankfully, my diagnosis had a misleading prognosis, and we have three precious children to show for it. But there are so many other times when a chapter of our life story didn't end well, yet the narrative of love and transparency carries us through.

Expectations

Expectations are a deep-seated part of who we are; we don't often think about them because we don't often notice them. But being aware of our relationship expectations gives us a chance to bring them to the surface in a constructive way. What are your views on work, family, gender, and marriage roles? How will you accomplish the cooking, the cleaning, and the chores? What do you "expect" or "assume" the role of a wife is in a relationship? What is the role of the husband? All of these underlying thoughts and beliefs make up your relationship expectations and the unspoken things you may simply assume because of how you were raised, what you saw growing up, or what you were taught to believe. This is just skimming the surface of the things we may expect going into marriage, and it is an important conversation to have.

> Being aware of our relationship expectations
> gives us a chance to bring them to the
> surface in a constructive way.

Money

It is amazing how a topic such as money can seem so benign before marriage and become such a trigger after marriage. Too many couples get caught in a trap of financial stress and struggles because they did not take the time to discuss finances. How do you feel about combining money? What are your spending habits? Do you have any debt, and how are you going to pay it off? What are your views on saving, tithing, and giving? Getting on the same page when it comes to money will save you much strain and heartache along the way.

I cohosted a podcast in which we talked through relationship issues related to love and money. In one episode, a newly engaged couple called in to talk through their spending differences. She valued taking care of herself, so for her, it was perfectly acceptable to spend 30 bucks on a bottle of shampoo. He was a penny-pincher who thought it was ridiculous to spend anything more than $1.99 when you could get an entire bottle of Suave 3-in-1 to cover all of your hygiene needs. Clearly, there was some disagreement about issues of finance, and they were calling us to help them decide who was right. But at the end of the day, there really is no winner or loser in these types of conversations, unless you go into relationships assuming instead of asking and communicating. The fact that they were already talking through these issues showed us that they were way ahead of the game. We have to learn to drop the cover in every aspect of the important topic of money.

Faith

Genuine faith is something that should be evident in your life long before you get married. But just as important as it is to retain your individual relationship with God, it is also important to connect in faith experiences and beliefs as a relationship begins to deepen and develop in the season of fall. Discussions about prayer life, reading God's Word, spiritual roles, theological beliefs, and denominational preferences are all things that need to be considered and discussed as you move forward. There can be no assumptions. You need to get real about your relationship with God and get comfortable with the process of exposing your beliefs and sharing your experiences.

Children

There is much more to the topic of family planning before marriage than dreaming about baby names. How many children do you want to have? What happens if you aren't able to get pregnant? How do you know when you are done having children? How were you parented, and what are your personal views on parenting? What do you believe about discipline, and are you on the same page with your perspectives? Who will primarily take care of the children, or will it always be a shared venture? What are your views on day care, schooling, and the like? There are many important aspects of this topic, and it would be beneficial to discuss and work through them with complete disclosure and honesty because this topic will impact your relationship from beginning to end.

Boundaries

Boundaries are your views on what is okay and what is not okay when it comes to your relationship and marriage. They are the limits that protect your relationship, keeping the good things in and the bad things out. The problem is that most couples talk through boundaries *after* something bad happens in the relationship instead of *before*. But boundaries are most protective when they are discussed long before an issue comes up. I worked with a couple that learned this the hard way. They went into marriage with a lot of assumptions about their relationship. Both identified as born-again Christians, and they assumed that nothing could harm their relationship and that they would always make good choices—even in times of stress. As a result, they didn't take the time to talk through what it looked like to protect their marriage when the hard things came along.

A couple years into their relationship, they found themselves dealing with some stressors that caused an emotional rift between them. Having never clearly talked through boundaries and limits, they found themselves making poor choices during that time of stress and frustration. He began binge-watching Netflix and shutting down emotionally as a way to deal with the stress, while she went out to socialize and flirt with her coworkers late into the night as her way of coping. They stopped spending time together, and they had no boundaries to keep their relationship intact. Eventually, his lack of boundaries from within coupled with her lack of boundaries from without led to her having an affair with a coworker. Their lack of boundaries opened the door for things to harm their marriage when they were the most susceptible.

They are still struggling to repair the damage that has been done to their relationship.

In the season of fall, you have to get really good at dropping the cover and talking through everything, even the things you never wish to experience. What do boundaries look like with friends of the opposite sex, past boyfriends or girlfriends, and even family members? How will you protect your time? How will you guard your emotions? How will you try to prevent your heart from negative or unhealthy interactions with others? Failing to talk through these topics will leave you susceptible to problems and broken trust along the way.

Sins and Struggles

Marriage is like a pressure cooker. In the context of such an intimate relationship, whatever you put into the pressure cooker of marriage gets intensified. Marriage intensifies your strengths, and it intensifies your weaknesses. That's why it is so important to be honest about your bad habits and hang-ups here and now. Do you tend to express anger through rage? Do you struggle with any addictive behaviors? Are there any areas in your life that you need to expose and address before you move toward marriage? Take the time to talk frankly and honestly about your struggles, and make the time to work toward hope and healing.

To get through the season of fall, you have to drop the facade. You have to come to terms with who you are and where you are going. You have to get comfortable with being uncomfortable, dropping your cover, and revealing your bare branches. You have to realize that the enemy of intimacy is assumption, but the ally of trust is truth.

> The enemy of intimacy is assumption,
> but the ally of trust is truth.

As I look out the window and watch the final few leaves drop to the ground, I realize that there is nowhere left to hide. The leaves are gone.

The branches are bare. The trees are exposed. But in their vulnerable state, I see an unspoken invitation: an invitation to be known, an invitation to be seen, and an invitation to come as you are.

Reflection Questions for Couples

1. There comes a point in each of our lives where we have to learn to "drop the cover" and expose the bare branches of our sins and struggles in order for us to begin to heal. Take some time to pray and ask God to reveal to you any areas in your life where you need to "drop the cover" in order to pursue healing.

2. Read through the list of Ten Things to Ask, Not Assume. Is there anything in your life that you haven't fully exposed to your spouse? Are there any areas where you are holding on to lies or refraining from sharing the truth?

3. What steps can you take to have important conversations and build (or rebuild) the chain of trust in your marriage?

Reflection Questions for Singles

1. There comes a point in each of our lives where we have to learn to "drop the cover" and expose the bare branches of our sins and struggles in order for us to begin to heal. Take some time to pray and ask God to reveal to you any areas in your life where you need to "drop the cover" in order to pursue healing.

2. Read through the list of Ten Things to Ask, Not Assume, and ask yourself: Do I have a trusted friend or mentor who knows about these aspects of my life? If not, what is keeping you from developing authentic relationships?

3. Has the "chain of trust" ever been broken by someone significant in your life? How might that experience impact your future relationships? Ask God to help you heal as you begin to believe that trust is something that must be earned, not freely given.

WINTER—LONG DAYS AHEAD

Winter is a time of settling down, preparing for the cold, long days ahead. The strong emotions that were once felt begin to cool as we settle into the normalcy and familiarity of day-to-day life. Winter is a necessary time—a quiet time to reflect on the changes that need to be made as we prepare for the things to come. There is a deep comfort that comes with the season of winter—but there is also a danger.

If we're not careful, we can get so comfortable in the predictability of this season that we lose our motivation and intentionality. In the season of winter, we can find ourselves vulnerable to the frostbite of apathy. The slow and quiet cooling of winter can cause us to forget, to stop pursuing the strong love and commitment we once had.

In winter, many couples find themselves dealing with the freeze—feeling stuck in their relationship, unable or unsure of how to take steps forward. Dealing with hurt, bitterness, or disconnect, it can feel like winter will last a lifetime.

But the season of winter is not meant to be stayed in; it's meant to be passed through. Seasons come, and seasons go, and if we're deliberate in taking the right steps and intentional in choosing the right actions, we will find that the thaw of winter is right around the corner, and the hope that spring will come again.

10

FROST—THE CHILL
OF APATHY

The first frost of the season comes quietly, unannounced—like a thief in the night. For most of us, waking up to frost on the ground is a mild inconvenience. It means that it is time to dig through our closets, pack up our light jackets, and pull out our heavy coats to prepare for the winter season. At worst, it might mean we have to run outside and scrape off a little of the fuzzy, velvet ice from our car's windshield before we head to work.

But for farmers, whose entire livelihoods rise and fall with the weather, an untimely frost can be detrimental. I read a heartbreaking story about an Australian farmer who lost 80 percent of his entire crop due to an untimely and unexpected frost.[1] One particular unexpected frost in Australia was referred to as the worst natural disaster to ever hit the local farmers of the area, killing up to 95 percent of the crops.[2] The frozen earth can kill roots that run deep, causing irreversible damage to crops, plants, and all kinds of vegetation. Frost has the power to kill as it quietly cools the ground, sending invisible shock waves into everything it touches.

There's a type of frost that happens in relationships as well—a cooling that comes in quietly, unannounced, like a thief in the night. It has the power to kill as it slowly seeps in, sending invisible shock waves into our hearts and into our relationships. It is the frost of apathy, and it is one of the quietest and most dangerous intruders.

Comfortably Cool

When I was engaged to John, a married friend of mine took me out for lunch to give me a pep talk about the reality check of married life. We had a candid talk about all kinds of things from sex to sleeping arrangements and bathroom habits. I'll never forget when she asked me if I could ever see myself using the bathroom in front of John when we were married. I remember naively responding, *"Never!"* Even though I felt totally comfortable around my husband-to-be, I couldn't imagine *that* level of comfort. It is one thing to imagine being intimate and affectionate in the bedroom, but it is a whole other thing to imagine chitchatting in the bathroom while someone is sitting on the porcelain throne. How unromantic! Fast-forward over ten years into marriage, and the joke's on me. It is not uncommon for either of us to shout out to the other from the bathroom, "Hey, hon! Come in here! I have something to tell you! Oh, and can you grab me a roll of toilet paper while you're at it?" The level of comfort that I have with my husband is so far beyond anything I ever could have imagined. We have far surpassed the bodily functions of the lavatory and plunged even deeper into the comfort levels of things such as giving birth (talk about bodily functions) and dealing with major sickness (where fluids are coming out of every orifice)! "Comfort" has taken on a whole new meaning in my book.

Every relationship goes through a season when the heightened emotions of spring and the passion of summer begin to cool off in the reality of everyday life. Despite what they try to get you to believe in Hollywood, the majority of life isn't actually romantic at all. Most of the interactions you will have in your relationship have very little to do with romance and sexual chemistry, and very much to do with the day-in, day-out process of real life.

Romance in a relationship isn't just about making out, planning special dates, writing elaborate notes, and buying chocolates and roses—it's also about making the bed, planning the weekly dinner menu, writing out the list of things that need to be done this week, and buying new lightbulbs at Home Depot. Passion in a relationship isn't just displayed with grand gestures of affection—it is also displayed in loading the dishwasher, running a load of laundry, getting the oil changed in the car, and remembering to pay the bills. Chemistry might be about emotions, but commitment—long-term commitment—is about actions. True love is fully displayed in the day-in, day-out actions of everyday life. There is a deep intimacy that comes within the framework of the normalcy of life and doing life together. But, if we are not careful, the deep comforts of doing life together can quietly morph into apathy.

> Romance isn't just about special dates,
> elaborate notes, chocolates and roses—it's
> also about making the bed, planning dinner,
> listing chores, and buying new lightbulbs.

The Chill of Apathy

As with all the other seasons of a relationship, there's no exact time frame for when a couple will reach the frost of winter. But for the majority of couples, it happens when they've been together for a few years. The higher the level of comfort, the more likely that the frost of winter will find its way into the relationship. I counseled a couple who had been dating for five years and were struggling with the apathy of winter. Looking at their relationship, there was very little that concerned them, outside of the fact that they were struggling with apathy. The excitement they used to feel in the very beginning of their relationship had been replaced with the expected. Every week brought with it the same interactions and exchanges. Each day of the week was mapped out with the same type of activities and interactions: a combination of work, life, family, and ministry. Having been together for so long, they had settled into the monotony and routine of real life, and the warm feelings of spring had cooled off into the familiar temperatures of winter.

Many couples experience a similar phenomenon at some point in their relationship. There's nothing majorly disturbing in their relationship, but then again, there's nothing majorly exciting either. Their relationship has gone from fiery to functional, and their daily interactions have less to do with love and more to do with living. They feel caught in apathy, going through the motions of a relationship without actually engaging in the relationship.

I remember when I first witnessed the problem of apathy in a relationship, but at that time in my life, I was on the outside looking in. John and I were newlyweds, and a few of our married friends had started having children. One evening, when we were all together on a couples' night out, I noticed a peculiar thing. Most of the couples in the group weren't holding hands or even sitting together. There was a lack of interaction between the married duos, which seemed absurd to me at the time; as a newly married couple, John and I could barely stand the thought of being seated apart. As I continued observing, a pattern emerged. There was a definite lack of physical touch, emotional expression, or affectionate interaction between the couples, which seeped into their everyday life. I remember thinking to myself, *We can never let this happen to us...*

Fast-forward a few years, when John and I now have two kids under two years of age. Our newlywed friends came over for dinner one evening, and the phenomenon repeated itself again right before my eyes—except this time, *we* were the apathetic couple. We were the ones sitting across the room from one another, passing babies back and forth, changing diapers in between conversations, and holding bottles and baby toys instead of holding hands, while our newlywed friends sat so romantically on the loveseat with hardly a centimeter of space between them. I started wondering, *Was this an isolated incident? When did it happen that we'd become so comfortable with separateness? When did our affections get displaced? Was this just part of the process of having little ones to care for, or had we actually let our relationship slip to the back burner? How were we relating to one another when the kids were not around? Were we being intentional to connect and deliberate to interact?*

The answers to those questions were complicated and layered. Part of it was certainly the normal wear and tear of raising a family. It is hard to be exchanging bedroom eyes while you are changing diapers. It is difficult to sit entangled in each other's arms when you are certain that the moment you get distracted, one of your children will likely try to stick a fork in the electrical outlet. Part of it was the normal strain that raising a family will put on a marriage. But part of it was our lack of effort and motivation to prioritize our love, to find new ways of showing affection, and to keep our relationship front and center. We weren't being intentional to fight against the apathy, and the frost of winter had quietly entered our home completely unannounced and unexpected.

For some couples, the sting of apathy goes unnoticed for quite some time. They can go on for months or years without ever realizing that they are experiencing a lack of connection, affection, and enthusiasm in their relationship. They do not even realize that their relationship has taken a backseat. They may spend the evenings sitting in the same room but hardly interacting because they are both staring at their phones or mindlessly watching Netflix. For others, the frostbite of apathy stings harder, and they find themselves completely aware that they are going through the motions of a relationship with feelings of discouragement, loneliness, and despair. They feel indifferent and detached. They find themselves disconnected from their partner, and they are not sure how to solve the problem because they don't know exactly what the problem is.

Dealing with the Frost

So how does a couple deal with the frost of winter? And if it is something that every couple will likely experience at some point, how can a couple be sure to *get through* the frost together rather than allowing it to become the norm?

#1: Identify the Root Cause

When you recognize that you are dealing with the frost of apathy, it may seem like it came out of nowhere, or, conversely, that it has always been this way. But neither is true. Apathy in a relationship happens over time, and for each step that led you away from each other, there's a step that can lead you back. The first step is identifying the root cause.

It may be hard to figure this out right away, and there may be many layers to the apathy you are feeling, but here are some key questions to consider as you begin to process your unique situation:

- Have you been prioritizing your emotional connection and communication?

- Has physical touch been a regular part of your relationship, and if you are married, has sexual intimacy been a regular part of your relationship?

- Are there any issues, conflicts, or problems that you are ignoring or failing to deal with?

- Are your lives too busy, causing you to neglect making time for one another and prioritizing your relationship?

- Could there be an underlying health concern, such as clinical depression, anxiety, a hormonal imbalance, or another medical problem that is impacting motivation and desire?

- Are you setting enough boundaries with other people so that you have enough emotional energy to invest in one another? And, if you are married with kids, are you setting enough boundaries with your children so that you have enough emotional energy to invest in one another?

Identifying the root cause of the issue has to be the first step so that you can come up with a plan to break the cycle of apathy.

#2: Discuss the Problem

Once you have identified what you think may be the root cause of the problem, make it a priority to let your partner know what you are noticing and experiencing in the relationship. Be careful not to point the finger at the other person; rather, make general observations and communicate your personal feelings and experiences. Ask a lot of questions, make it your main goal to learn how your partner is experiencing the relationship, and listen for any concerns they might have. Talk through some of these questions together:

- What's something we each love about our relationship?

- What's one thing we wish we could work on or change about our relationship?

- Which of the things from the "root list" above could be something we're dealing with in our relationship or in our individual lives?

- Are there any issues or conflicts that we've been unwilling or unable to resolve?

- Is there anything we need to carve out of our life, or any places where we need to set boundaries in order to have time to make our relationship a priority?

- How can we integrate more time for conversation, emotional connection, and physical touch in our relationship?

Let the goal of this conversation be to listen and learn. There are no right or wrong answers, just an opportunity to connect with the goal of working through the frost of apathy.

#3: Come Up with a Plan of Action

Once you have discussed these questions, it is time to come up with a tangible plan. It is not enough to chat through it, say "good talk," and move on with life doing the same things over. You have to actually make a plan and start to implement that plan. This is where too many people fall short in the cycle of change because they never get to this crucial step. We all say we want things to change, yet taking the steps to make things happen is the hardest part. But you cannot lose weight without working out and eating right. You cannot fix your car without actually getting under the hood or taking it to a mechanic. You cannot get a degree without picking up a book and studying. And you cannot get through relationship problems without actually doing the work. So, let's start with small steps and think through how you'll do things differently:

- What is one thing you will do to increase affection and

physical touch in your relationship over the next three months?

- How do you plan on making time for communication this coming week? Can you come up with a practical plan to communicate regularly long term? Are you willing to put it on the calendar and write it in the schedule?

- Do you need to make an appointment with a counselor, a medical doctor, or a healthcare practitioner to take a baby step toward fixing a root issue?

- List one or two things you need to take out of your life to make more time for your relationship.

- Is there anyone specific with whom you need to set a boundary, and what will that boundary be?

- What's something you can do to increase romance this coming week?

Your action plan is the one and only thing that can begin the process of melting away the frost of apathy in your relationship, helping you to get through the season of winter.

Frost in Dating

I want to take a moment to address those of you who are dating and find yourself struggling through the frost of winter. As I mentioned earlier, apathy in a relationship can occur at different times, but the longer you've been together, the more likely it is. But what if you've been dating someone for a short period of time, and you are already struggling with feelings of apathy and disconnection? If that is the case, go back and read through the section of this book about spring, and ask yourself, *Is the problem in the relationship? Or is the problem in me?*

In other words, is there something in your relationship that is causing you to feel an indifference and disconnection this early on? Is there an underlying issue preventing you from connecting to your partner and building an emotional connection? Or is the problem coming from within? Are there unaddressed issues in your past, fears of commitment, or trust issues that you may be facing? Dealing with frost early on in a relationship is a clear sign that there is a problem that needs to be addressed. In some cases, when the problem is coming from within, there's often a solution and a way to move forward because healing from within often brings healing to your relationship. But in other cases, when there are unresolvable issues in the relationship or a lack of compatibility, it is important to consider that frost this early may be a sign that this relationship is not a good match.

Back in college I dated a guy and within a couple months quickly found myself struggling with the frost of apathy. I didn't know why I had such a lack of motivation or desire to keep the relationship growing. I was missing the excitement and joy that I knew I should be feeling in the beginning of a relationship. Instead of experiencing the season of spring, I felt like the relationship started in the season of winter. I was confused and wondered if I was somehow doing something wrong and even questioned if my expectations were realistic.

It took me some time, but I eventually realized that my strong feelings of apathy this early on and this consistently in the dating relationship were pointing to a bigger problem that I needed to address sooner than later. I decided I needed to step back from the relationship, to consider whether the problem was in me or in the relationship. Over the next few months, God revealed to me that the answer was a little bit of both. As God began to work in my heart and heal me from the inside out, I also realized there were many things about this relationship that I was settling for when it came to matters of faith, personality, and compatibility. The frost of apathy was pointing to something deeper that I had not been willing to address while I was in the relationship. Stepping back gave me the distance and space I needed to see that this relationship was not right for me and freed me to move forward, trusting God would lead me through the four seasons of a relationship in the right time and with the right person. I'm so glad I allowed myself to take that step, because letting go of a relationship that was not a good match for me opened my heart to meeting John many years later and to fully experiencing a relationship that was the very best match for me.

Cozying Up

A few days ago, John and I finally succumbed to the impulse to turn on the heat in our home, which for me is a no-turning-back sign that winter is upon us. The days are getting longer and darker with each passing hour. The weather is getting colder and colder. Clearing frost off the windshield has become a regular part of the daily routine, and my weather app even tells me that there's snow in the forecast. I guess it is time to finally accept the fact that winter is here—and maybe even learn to enjoy it.

Last night, John and I snuggled up together on the couch under my favorite king-sized gray blanket, with the sweet smell of my pine-scented candle drifting in the air from earlier that day. Winter is perfect for cuddling. With it being so dark outside, we decided to put the kids to bed early and cozy up together to watch a movie. I had just washed my hair, and my wild natural curls were all over the place, my face without a spot of makeup, and I was wearing my most comfortable baggy pajamas. We looked over at each other, in the absolute comfort of our relationship, and exchanged a really good kiss. John always tells me that I look most attractive to him in my "natural state"—when my hair is undone and my face a blank canvas. I certainly don't see it, but I'm sure glad he does. You see, there is also unmatched beauty in the familiar and unsurpassed security in the expected. There's comfort in a relationship where you are so well known, yet so well loved. So, brace yourselves because winter is here. And you might as well learn to make the most of it.

Reflection Questions for Couples

1. In what ways has the frost of apathy impacted your relationship? Take some time to discuss this chapter and hear each other's feedback regarding apathy.

2. List some ways that you can deal with the frost in your relationship.

3. Together, come up with a plan of action to help you rekindle the romance and affection in your marriage.

Reflection Questions for Singles

1. Have you witnessed the frost of apathy impacting the relationships of anyone you know? What were some signs that this might be the case?

2. Have you ever found yourself dealing with the frost of apathy in a dating relationship? How did this play out? Were you able to identify if the problem was coming from the relationship, or if the problem was something you were personally struggling with?

3. What are some action steps you would like to take in your future relationship to prevent the "frost of apathy"?

11

FREEZE—STUCK IN LOVE

I didn't know the meaning of winter until I moved to Illinois.

After we were married, I packed up my things and joined John in his frigid state, where temperatures commonly hit below zero in the wintertime. I had no clue it could get so cold. I spent five years living in Virginia, where winter is mild and a dusting of snow on the ground closes down businesses and brings everything to a halt. But in Illinois, there's no such thing as a dusting of snow. You have to have at least six inches on the ground before anyone considers calling it quits. The level of freeze that takes place in the subzero temperatures is something that took me a while to get used to. I remember many winter mornings going out to a dead car because it was so cold that my car wouldn't start. Winter can have that effect on things. It can have that kind of effect on relationships as well.

The Freeze

As a professional counselor, I have seen the impact that the season of winter can have on relationships. It can freeze a relationship to the point that it is unrecognizable. The emotional temperature between two people can feel so cold and frigid that they start wondering if it is even possible for it to ever warm up again. They find that the strong connection they used to feel has been replaced by separation and distance. The joy and laughter that used to permeate their relationship is now marked by arguments and tension.

For some couples, the temperature of their relationship is so cold that it starts to impact those around them. Anyone in close proximity can literally feel the emotional ice. I knew a couple whose relationship was so cold that they might as well have had icicles dangling off their noses. You could just feel the frigid tension between them as they shot frosty looks at one another and exchanged cold remarks back and forth. It is one thing to be frustrated with your spouse in private, but it is a whole other thing to allow that frustration into the public arena. But every time we were around them, it was inevitable. She was constantly cutting him down and criticizing him in front of everyone. She belittled him, nagged him, and picked him apart on a regular basis. Not only was it sad to witness the breakdown of a relationship in this way, it was awkward to be around them. The ice-cold tension in their relationship made everyone else feel uncomfortable. But feeling awkward or uncomfortable is the least of our concerns when it comes to observing the freeze of winter because in a marriage or relationship where children are involved, feeling the unrelenting freeze of a relationship can be detrimental for a child.

We learn so much about love based on how love is communicated in our family of origin. How a child witnesses relationships in his or her family of origin influences the way a child will engage in relationships later on in his or her adult life. As a mother of three children, this is a constant reminder for me, a built-in accountability factor for how I am choosing to relate to my husband on a regular basis. We have little eyes watching us, forming their view of life, love, commitment, and relationships. We owe it not only to ourselves to make sure we are modeling healthy relationships, but we also owe it to them and to future generations.

For some couples, the freeze of their relationship impacts those around them. But for other couples, the freeze of their relationship goes unnoticed by others yet is devastatingly obvious to themselves. They might feel frozen on the inside, but they bundle up tight so that no one would ever notice from the outside looking in. They get really good at putting on a smile and pretending that everything is fine in their relationship or in their marriage, when really, everything is as far as possible from being "fine."

Jeff and Danielle

Jeff and Danielle were struggling in the freeze of winter. It had probably been that way for years. But they were so used to the cold that they didn't even bother to address it anymore. They both came from families where their parents' marriages ended either in divorce or lifelong apathy, so their assumption was that this must be what marriage looks like after 15 years. Year by year, they had slowly drifted apart emotionally, spiritually, and physically. When they were together, they were good at putting on a show, projecting to outsiders that everything was fine. Their family and friends had no idea that they were sleeping in separate rooms, involved in separate activities, and barely interacting with each other. Their schedules were completely opposite, like two ships passing in the night. Worse yet, their love and affection toward one another had frozen over.

Bitter Cold

Like Jeff and Danielle, in some relationships, the freeze takes an unexpected form. It doesn't come with yelling, screaming, and fits of anger like most people would expect. It comes with a quiet, unmistakable chill—the cold shoulder, the avoidance of eye contact, the withholding of physical touch. The withdrawal of affection. The lack of conversation and communication. The gradual separation of space, time, and activities. Two people, living under one roof, who shared nothing but empty glances and hollow words.

Icy Hot

In other relationships, the freeze of winter packs its own heat. Instead of cooling down in the tension of their relationship, they find themselves heating up in stress and frustration. They feel stuck in a cycle of constant arguing, heated conflict, and heightened emotions of anger, rage, and bitterness. Conversations seem to escalate and trying to deal with conflict feels like going around and around in circles with nothing to show for it but high blood pressure, broken objects, and tear-stained cheeks. Arguments get so bad that they find themselves exchanging terrible words or acting in irrational ways. Like the wife who got so angry that she shattered every glass cup in the china cabinet. Or the husband who felt so unnerved that he threatened to leave and never come back as he slammed the door behind him. If we aren't careful, the freeze of winter can leave us with more than shattered china cups. It can leave us with shattered hearts and broken lives.

Stuck in Love

Anyone in a significant relationship can tell you that relationships have the power to make you rise, but they also have the power to make you fall. They can build you up, but they can also tear you down. When you are struggling in your relationship, you can find yourself struggling in everything else as well. Feeling stuck in a relationship can affect your career, your emotional well-being, and even your physical health. While there can be many things at play in the deep freeze of winter, here are a few signs that your relationship needs some attention.

- You find that you feel more bitterness than affection toward your partner.

- You spend more time arguing than you do connecting.

- Your disagreements escalate, and you end with more conflict rather than with resolution.

- You feel more like strangers than friends.

- You can go for weeks or months without touching or connecting physically.

- You feel more emotionally drained than filled after being together.

- You find that you never disagree about anything because you hardly interact (this tells me that real needs and desires aren't being expressed on a regular basis, and that feelings of passivity and/or safety need to be explored).

- You're so busy and distracted that you have less than 30 minutes of quality conversation in a week.

- You feel disconnected and not "in tune" with one another emotionally or spiritually.

- You find that you are clueless about your partner's activities, interactions, and behaviors when you are not around.

- You have unresolved issues from the past that keep coming up again and again to haunt your relationship in the present.

- You would much prefer to spend your free time with someone other than your partner.

- You find yourself entertaining thoughts of being with someone else.

If you are struggling with one or more of the above, it is important to remember that while winter may last a season, it is not meant to last a lifetime. If you have been stuck in the grip of winter for more than a few months, you have to come up with a plan of action in order to begin to melt away the freeze. Most couples will experience the season of winter at some point throughout the lifetime of their relationship, but winter is meant to be passed through, not stayed in. It's meant to be a season, not a permanent state.

Even in the Arctic

In a homeschool lesson with my kids, I was reading to them about the many different climates around our world. The Arctic was one of the climates we spent some time studying, where it is basically winter all year round. What's interesting about the Arctic is that it is actually considered a desert because such little precipitation occurs in the frigid temperatures. In fact, it gets about the same amount of precipitation as the Sahara desert. With such little precipitation and such cold temperatures, very little wildlife and plant life survive in this type of environment.

Because such little vegetation grows in these areas, the people who live here have to pay a fortune to import fruits and vegetables. The lack of healthy vegetables, fruits, and grains had severely impacted the health and well-being of the residents of these areas. They were desperate for a solution to feed their children and take control of their health. So, they decided to do something about it. They built a greenhouse in the middle of the Arctic!

They found an abandoned ice hockey rink and repurposed it as a giant greenhouse. With a lot of help, hard work, and a commitment of time and energy, the greenhouse has become a source of sustenance and joy for the entire community. "It might sound cheesy," said one of the greenhouse's assistant coordinators, "but it's a testimony of hope that you can do something if you want to, even in the frozen Arctic."[1]

This story is a hopeful reminder that no matter how dire your situation, there is always a next step to take. Even in the frozen tundra of a relationship that seems stuck in the grip of winter, there is always a choice to be made of whether you'll choose to give up in the impossibility of it all or choose to move forward with actions of hope.

"Moving Forward" Does Not Mean What You Think

When you hear the words "move forward," you most likely assume that I am referring to an attempt to restore and heal a relationship. But that is not always the healthiest option in every situation. There is no such thing as a one-size-fits-all approach to relationships, and moving forward looks different in every relationship.

Moving Forward in Marriage

For those of you who are married, this chapter may have struck a painful nerve. You might find yourself struggling through some or all of the aspects of the freeze of winter. Marriage is, above all else, a covenant relationship between two people, made to point to God and His love for us through its unmistakable example of permanence and unconditional love. God wants your marriage to succeed. Though He sees the deep pain that the freeze of a relationship can bring, He also sees the deep, deep love that can be found on the other side of winter—a love that can point you to God like few things can.

I believe that the enemy longs to keep our marriages stuck in the freeze of winter because that is when our marriages become the least effective at showing God's love to the world. When we are stuck in love, we'll find that we are stuck in so many other areas of our life: We are stuck in an inability to parent well, an inability to serve others well, an inability to give and to love and to pour into others. Feeling paralyzed in our marriage will ultimately paralyze us and keep us from living life the way it was meant to be lived.

It is important for us to recognize the spiritual significance of being stuck in love and understand our role in healing our relationship. In every relationship that is stuck in love, there are two people who are feeling stuck in their individual lives as well. It is so easy to see and point out the flaws of our spouse and the areas they need to change, but doing so inhibits healing. It simply doesn't work. Taking steps to heal spiritually, emotionally, and psychologically in our individual lives will be the one and only thing that will eventually impact our marriages. Whether or not we feel it, in marriage we are completely interconnected with our spouse. We're like two gears on a watch, linked together with grooves and notches like 100 pieces of a puzzle. When one of us moves forward in our personal life, we'll find our relationship begins to move as well—it has to.

> In every relationship that is stuck in love, there are two people who are feeling stuck in their individual lives as well.

Have you been so stuck in the freeze of winter that you've stopped moving forward? Have you been so paralyzed by the bitter cold of this season that you've decided to "stay in winter" rather than trek through it? It can be hard to take steps forward, and at times, it can even feel impossible, but the work of relationships is always worth the work of love that God can do in you and through you as you choose to move forward in healing. You don't have to feel it to believe it; in fact, few people "feel it" in the frost of this season. But you have to choose to move forward in faith, believing that the power of God has the ability to thaw even the most frozen hearts. What is the next step for you? How can you begin to move forward, even today? As you read through the list below, ask God if there are any areas you need to change in your life that will ultimately begin to bring needed change to your relationship:

- Do I need to work on getting to the root of my emotions so that I can control them?

- Do I need to carve out space in my day for God and His Word?

- Do I need to commit to praying for my marriage on a regular basis?

- Do I need to deal with any issues from my past that are impacting me?

- Do I need to learn how to express my emotions and needs in a healthy way?

- Do I need to set more boundaries and limits in my life or in my marriage?

- Do I need to get better at showing love to my spouse through increased physical touch, words of affirmation, acts of service, quality time, or thoughtful gifts?[2]

- Do I need to become a better listener and respond to my spouse's needs?

- Do I need to be quick to encourage and slow to criticize instead of the opposite?

- Do I recognize the personal sins and struggles I need to deal with in my own life?

- What else could God be prompting me to change in my life and in my heart?

Making Changes

In the freeze of winter, it is not enough to simply want change or to recognize the need for change. We have to take steps toward change. Lasting change is a product of time, deliberate energy, hard work, and seeking help. Seeking help is an overlooked part of relationships and marriage in general. Unfortunately, people don't usually come to me for counseling until *after* their relationship is in trouble. But counseling needs to be a part of the active maintenance of a relationship. Counseling is like preventative maintenance. You don't take a car to get an oil change *after* it breaks down. Neither should you seek counseling *after* the relationship fails, as a last-ditch effort for change.

Growing in love and pursuing change must be built into the framework of your life from the beginning to the end. There is no better time to start than now, through the process of professional counseling. Counseling provides a beautiful and remarkable journey of getting to know yourself in a way you may never have thought you could. I think every individual person needs to find a Christian licensed counselor and commit to a series of at least six to eight counseling sessions in pursuit of getting yourself healthy and whole. Even if your partner does not want to come with you, do not let that prevent you from taking steps for yourself. Healthy people make healthy relationships, and there is no better time and no better place to start becoming healthy in your life than right here and right now. Becoming healthy will never be in vain.

Moving Forward in a Toxic Marriage

Now let me take some time to specifically address those of you who find yourself in a toxic relationship. Given the nature of toxic relationships, there's a good chance that the person perpetuating most of the toxicity in the marriage is not the one reading this book. With that in mind, I'm primarily going to address the person on the receiving end of the toxicity. You might be reading this chapter in light of a dysfunctional marriage: a marriage in which you are suffering through abuse, dealing with your or your spouse's addictive behaviors, or even facing the sting of adultery or abandonment. First and foremost, my heart breaks for you. This was never God's design for marriage, and when His people are hurting in relationships, His heart hurts too. When God says that He "hate[s] divorce" (Malachi 2:16 NASB), it is because He knows the type of pain and devastation that a toxic marriage can inflict upon His children, and He doesn't want any of us to have to walk through that depth of heartache.

If you are dealing with the pain of a toxic marriage, I want to encourage you to see the importance of taking care of yourself because when you are not well, your relationships have no hope of being well. For you, taking care of yourself means getting yourself to a safe place and surrounding yourself with safe people who can support you, encourage you, speak truth to your heart, and help you set boundaries in your life and in your relationship. There is so much involved in unpacking the layers of a toxic relationship, and it is a process you cannot and should not do on your own. You need the love of a healthy community and the support of a professional counselor to walk with you through every step of the journey.

For most people in toxic relationships, especially within the Christian culture, the tendency is to stay quiet and move forward as a martyr. But God doesn't call us to secrecy; He calls us to freedom and redemption. Staying silent will only continue the unhealthy cycle and prevent you from reaching true freedom. The enemy wants you to keep things in the darkness because it is in the dark that sin continues to grow. God's Word encourages us to "have nothing to do with the fruitless deeds of darkness, but rather expose them. It is shameful even to mention what the disobedient do in secret. But everything exposed by the light becomes visible—and everything that is illuminated becomes a light" (Ephesians 5:11-13). Bringing things into the light allows for the hope of healing to take place in your life and, in some cases, even in your relationship.

Find someone whom you can talk to today. Begin to process what you've gone through and come up with a plan for healing. Moving forward toward your personal safety and well-being will give you the strength you need to identify what brought you to this place and how you can get to a better place. We serve a God of redemption, and no matter what it is you are going through, God can redeem it! I cannot guarantee you that your relationship will be restored, but I can guarantee you that as you move forward and trust God with your healing, He will redeem all things. He takes our hurts, hardships, and failures and works all things for the good of those who love Him (Romans 8:28).

Moving Forward in Dating

Lastly, I want to take the time to address those of you who are reading this chapter through the lens of a dating relationship. In dating relationships, the season of winter can take on a different meaning than in marriage. In dating, winter should be a time of settling down and settling in. Your emotions might have cooled off from the intensity of spring, and you are finally starting to settle in to the day-in, day-out routine of life, getting a glimpse of what "doing life together" actually looks like. The fast-paced affections of spring have slowed to the mundane monotony of real life. This can be a really great thing for a relationship because it is a glimpse into "lifelong." Even in the mundane, a dating couple may find that their relationship is still strong, and they feel connected in a deeper way. They have gone through the hard things of life together, and they have survived the cold winter months side by side. Their worlds continue growing together, and they find themselves moving into an even deeper phase of their relationship as they look ahead to combining their lives and planning for marriage. If they can get through winter, they can certainly get through anything that life will throw their way.

But for other dating couples, winter ends with an entirely different conclusion. They find that the routine and normalcy of life starts to drown out their relationship. They start feeling a coldness toward one another, and their days become filled with tension, conflict, and frustration. They have not been able to communicate well or to navigate conflict well, and they start moving backward rather than forward. Instead of drawing together in the cold winter months, they start moving apart. They start reflecting on the past seasons—spring, summer, and fall—realizing that there are key ingredients missing in their relationship. They recognize that there are unhealthy traits and behaviors that aren't going to magically "go away." In winter, they find themselves coming to terms with the reality that things are not how they should be. Unable to make it through the freeze of winter, they acknowledge that their relationship has frozen over, and they make the decision to part ways.

The season of winter is so important in dating because it is the time to take inventory of the relationship and make sure that everything is as it should be before moving forward. What you see in the winter season of dating is ultimately what you will see intensified in marriage.

An Invitation to Leave

I love socializing, and so when I invite my closest friends over to my home, I make it a point to let them know that they can feel free to stay as long as they want. Come for coffee, stay for lunch, and if you feel led, by all means let's have dinner together too! Come for the day, and if you feel up for it, bring your pajamas and spend the weekend as well!

But I'm not this flexible around the clock. Even though I love socializing, I'm actually a "no" person by default, and setting boundaries around my life and family and time are important to me. So, if we are in a season where we have too much on the calendar, or we've committed to a few important things, I'm also just as quick to let people know what *won't* work regarding our time commitments. For example, when I'm in writing season like I am right now, my closest friends also know that if they are invited to come for coffee in the morning, that means everyone has to be heading out by 2 p.m. because that's always when I sit down to write. That also means on Saturday mornings I'm not going to be available until my book gets finished. There are seasons in my life when people are welcome to stay as long as they would like, but then there are other seasons in my life when they are also encouraged to leave.

The same goes with the seasons of a relationship. Some seasons call us to stay, to enjoy the blooming affection and deliberate planting of spring, to experience the heated passion and creative romance of summer, or to engage in the ongoing conversation and important communication of fall. Stay as long as you would like. Savor this season. Learn from this season. Enjoy this season.

But in the season of winter, things get turned upside down because the invitation is not to stay—the invitation is to leave. Winter is meant to be passed through, not stayed in. It is meant to bring things to light that we need to change, areas in which we need to grow, and things we need to work through on the way to the other side. Winter is a season that we cannot get too comfortable in because it is not meant to last long. If you find yourself stuck in the season of winter, let me encourage you that no matter what your situation, the choices you make today will pave the way for tomorrow—the way for hope, peace, reconciliation, and freedom. Winter is not meant as a final, permanent state because by the grace of God, there is a brighter season ahead.

> Winter is meant to be passed through, not stayed in.

Reflection Questions for Couples

1. Read through the list of warning signs of being "stuck in love." Have you ever experienced this type of winter freeze in your relationship?

2. When you struggle, is it typically bitter cold (withdrawal and a lack of emotional interaction), or icy hot (tense, loud, and argumentative)?

3. If you find yourself stuck in the freeze of winter, read through the list of steps to move forward and ask yourself, "What's one thing I can do to move forward today?"

Reflection Questions for Singles

1. Have you ever found yourself holding on to a dating relationship that had frozen over? What kept you from holding on rather than letting go?

2. When you deal with conflict in a friendship or relationship, do you tend to be bitter cold (withdrawing and stopping emotional connection), or icy hot (displaying obvious tension, heightened emotions, and arguing)?

12

THE THAW—SPRING WILL COME AGAIN

ave you ever noticed that some seasons fly by, while other seasons seem like they are going to last a lifetime? For John and me, summer is one of those seasons that flies by. One moment, we're celebrating the start of summer break: We're pulling out the flip-flops, getting vacations planned, traveling to the beach, and eating ice cream like it's a food group of its own. And then, somehow, we blink, and summer is instantly over: We're putting the swimsuits away, getting the back-to-school shopping done, going back to work, and bundling up for the cold. I find it rather depressing how fast summer goes by.

But then other seasons feel eternal, epic, limitless. Around here, winter is one of those "lifetime" seasons, especially the past few winters. The winter before last, it felt like we had so much snow that it would never melt. In fact, in one 24-hour period, it snowed over 36 inches. We were stuck at home for three days because there weren't enough snowplows to clear the streets. They were using emergency vehicles just to get people to work because the roads were so bad. That year, winter felt like it was about two years long.

Similarly, last winter, I was almost positive that it would still be snowing in June because winter just kept coming, and coming, and coming. In fact, I was scheduled to speak at an event near the end of March that ended up getting canceled due to a blizzard. Some seasons just don't want to say goodbye, whether or not they are welcome. Yet, no matter how epic a season might feel, at the end of the day, we know one thing for sure: Seasons only last for a season.

Seasons only last for a season.

Seasons Come, and Seasons Go

In the Song of Solomon, King Solomon reminds us that seasons come, and seasons go, and that different seasons bring with them different experiences. No matter what we are going through in life, we can walk through it knowing one thing for sure: The next season will replace the current season, which will then be overshadowed by the season after that.

There is a time for everything, and a season for every activity under the heavens:

a time to be born and a time to die,
a time to plant and a time to uproot,
a time to kill and a time to heal,
a time to tear down and a time to build,
a time to weep and a time to laugh,
a time to mourn and a time to dance,
a time to scatter stones and a time to gather them,
a time to embrace and a time to refrain from embracing,
a time to search and a time to give up,
a time to keep and a time to throw away,
a time to tear and a time to mend,
a time to be silent and a time to speak,
a time to love and a time to hate,
a time for war and a time for peace (Ecclesiastes 3:1-8).

While we are in this world, seasons will come, and seasons will go. I find that especially meaningful when I'm going through a difficult season of life. A few years ago, I walked through some of the hardest and most traumatic things I've ever experienced. I was going through a combination of significant health issues, fatigue from a brand-new baby, as well as dealing with an unexpected family crisis. The days felt long and dark, and I felt weary. In the middle of a really hard season, it's easy to start believing that it is never going to end. The season feels so limitless, so endless. When you don't see the light at the end of the tunnel, you can stop believing that the light even exists. You wonder if there's any way out.

You might be walking through a hard season right now, whether it be in your personal life or in your relationship. Sometimes one can lead to another. You might be tired, discouraged, and feeling like you have nothing left to give. The days feel dark, and the hours seem long. Maybe the darkness of winter has lasted so long that you've stopped believing that the light even exists. But I am here to remind you of this one thing: Seasons come, and seasons go. Spring will always come again.

Chilling Time

It is hard to believe that winter can be beneficial, much less have a purpose. But there is an unseen purpose to the cold, harsh months. In nature, the season of winter is extremely important to farmers across the country because it is during this season that the freezing temperatures eliminate many harmful insects and pathogens.[1] It is also the time of year when plants go into hibernation, reserving their energy for the season to come. Farmers call this a plant's "chilling time," noting that "without sufficient chilling time, a fruit tree will generate fewer, weaker buds, limiting fruit production from day one."[2]

Something similar happens through the season of winter in our own lives. As cold, harsh, and bitter as this season can feel in life and in relationships, deep down something is happening beyond what we can see. Maybe winter is a time of chilling for us, as well—a time when we are given the opportunity to recognize and eliminate the harmful things from our lives. What if, when we are feeling the paralysis of winter, God is asking us to rest in Him, to reserve our energy by relying on His strength, trusting that He is working in ways that we cannot know or even fathom? Nothing in our lives is wasted in the hands of Almighty God who can restore and redeem all things. I cling to the reminder that even in the hard seasons of our lives, He is making all things new: "Forget the former things; do not dwell on the past. See, I am doing a new thing! Now it springs up; do you not perceive it? I am making a way in the wilderness and streams in the wasteland" (Isaiah 43:18-19). The roles and responsibilities in this verse are incredibly clear: Our job is to move forward, to "not dwell on the past"; His job is to make a way in the wilderness.

Our Role

When it comes to relationships, we tend to take a passive role. I think we often default to the mentality that trusting God means we "do nothing" and wait for Him to do what He's going to do. But trusting God with our relationships doesn't mean that we don't take action; on the contrary, it means just the opposite—it means we trust Him enough to take action, even when it's hard.

We trust God, yet take responsibility in many other areas of our life. When we are on the hunt for work, we scour the internet researching job opportunities, send in our applications, and schedule multiple interviews. When we want to pursue further education, we pour in tons of money, read hundreds of books, study as hard as we can, and complete our assignments one by one until we graduate and receive our degree. When we are trying to get out of debt, we come up with a budget, plan out our spending, and figure out ways to make extra money so we can pay it off as fast as possible. We play an active role in so many other areas of our life, but when it comes to our love lives— one of the *most* important areas of our life—we tend to sit back, just hoping and praying that God will do the miraculous work of creating a healthy relationship for us.

But it doesn't work that way. Trusting God goes hand in hand with the choices we make on a daily basis, and those choices will either lead us toward love or push us away from love. No matter what season of a relationship you find yourself in today, the questions you need to ask yourself is this: "What is my responsibility in this season? What can I do to move myself toward healthy relationships? How can I 'forget the former things' and move toward what is ahead? What does it look like for me to take the next step in moving toward spring, as I continue to trust in what God is doing behind the scenes?" Trusting God and taking action go hand in hand. When we take action, we are openly demonstrating that we trust God because it takes so much trust to move forward, to make the next right choice, to take one step at a time, long before we know what's to come.

The Thaw of Spring

John and I openly talk about the difficult season that we walked through a few years into our marriage. It was the hardest year we had ever faced as a couple. John was working just under 100 hours per week as a resident, training to get his medical degree. We had just had our second child, and I was walking through the pit of postpartum depression. I was struggling with depression, anxiety, and insomnia all at once and trying to adjust to being a stay-at-home mom with two kids under the age of two. On top of all this, our extended family was going through a major hardship that was casting yet another shadow over our already dark season. The days felt long and burdensome. John and I were both feeling empty, but instead of recognizing our emptiness and finding healthy ways to get filled up, we both started isolating from each other in our own ways. After months of battling through this cold winter season, everything finally came to a head one night after a rather heated argument in which we both "imploded" beneath the weight of our struggle.

As we look back over a decade of marriage at that defining night, we are so grateful for that hard, chilling season of winter because it was that season that revealed to us the harmful "pathogens" in our own lives that we needed to eliminate. Each of us was caught in a cycle of coping with stress and struggles in a way that was causing more harm than good to ourselves and to our relationship. With tears in our eyes and pain in our hearts, we confessed, communicated, opened up, and began the process of forgiveness. We came up with a plan for how we would move forward and set up barriers to keep us from going back to our harmful ways of coping. We sought out mentorship and accountability and brought a few trusted others into our struggle so that we weren't facing it alone. And by God's grace, one day at a time, we started moving away from the past and began to move forward—out of the harshness of winter and into the warmth of spring.

I truly believe that the hardships of winter allowed us to move into a warmer season of spring than we had ever experienced before. As we took steps toward becoming healthier, living lives of complete transparency and prioritizing our relationship, our intimacy reached levels we never imagined possible. The harsh winter opened the door to experiencing spring in a way that was even better than the first time around. This is why I'm not afraid of the season of winter. Winter is a season that I believe every single married couple will go through again and again to varying degrees. But when we can begin to see each pass-through of winter as an opportunity, we allow it to strengthen rather than destroy us. We allow it to define us, to refine us, and to remake us. We invite it to transform us and to change us. Each time we are able to do that, we find that the thaw of spring is closer than it ever was before.

> When we can begin to see each pass-through
> of winter as an opportunity, we allow it to
> strengthen rather than destroy us.

Love in Every Season

As I write the final words of this chapter and watch this book come to a close, I can't help but find myself thinking of you—the reader of these words etched on this page. You could be so many things. You could be reading from any part of the country or even anywhere in the world. You could be single, dating, engaged, or married. You could be walking through a season of struggle or a season of joy. You could be in a time of loneliness or a time of intimacy. You could be walking through the bitter cold of winter, the complex colors of fall, the heat and passion of summer, or the planting and growing of spring. I can't help but wonder what kind of season you are journeying through today, and from the bottom of my heart, I wish I could hear every single one of your stories.

But while I may not know your unique journey or the things that you have walked through, I do know one thing: No matter where the journey of life has brought you, there is the ultimate hope of finding love in every season, a love that never fails. The deep love of God is the binding that holds every season together and the compass that keeps us moving in the right direction. It is the love that stays, the love that remains, the love that guides, and the love that cannot be washed away or undone. When we root our hearts in the unconditional love of God, we can walk through the seasons of love with confidence, knowing that no matter what life might bring our way, we'll never be separated from Love.

"For I am convinced that neither death nor life, neither angels nor demons, neither the present nor the future, nor any powers, neither height nor depth, nor anything else in all creation, will be able to separate us from the love of God that is in Christ Jesus our Lord" (Romans 8:38–39). It is the knowledge of that deep love that compels us to move forward as we walk through each season that life brings our way. When we experience His love, we are able to learn what it means to truly love others (John 13:34). It is in the reality of His love that we can be freed to love in every season.

While earthly love in this world is a gift we all seek, it's not guaranteed. We live in a broken world, which ultimately means that broken hearts, broken lives, broken dreams, and broken plans are oftentimes the by-product. When you've been looking for love in every season and haven't yet found it, you can start questioning if love even exists. I think of those of you who might be reading this book as older singles in your forties, fifties, or even in your sixties and beyond. Maybe you've been hoping for love, but obstacles in life have kept you from experiencing earthly love. Maybe you were married yet find yourself walking through the troubles and trials of divorce or the tragedy and sorrow of the death of a spouse. Maybe you are in a marriage in which you are struggling to believe that love can come again. Maybe you are wondering if it is even possible for you to find love in your life right now.

My encouragement to you is simply this: Be faithful to the role God has given you today, and trust Him to be faithful with His role. *Your job is only to move forward; His job is to make a way in the wilderness.* God's job is to make streams in the desert, and to make a way where there seems to be no way. His love for you is so deep, so wide, so high, so vast. If we could only catch a glimpse of His love for us, it would compel us to remain faithful and open our eyes to the love we can experience along the journey, no matter what season of life we might be in.

My dear friends, as you faithfully and deliberately journey through the four seasons of love, my final prayer for you is that you would know His love deeply, that you would feel Him close, and that His love would compel you and move you forward in loving others well. "God *is* love," and to know God is to know love (1 John 4:8). My desire is that you would know and believe with all your heart that no matter the season, Love is present, Love is constant, Love will be there. And even when you've yet to find love, may your eyes be opened to the reality that *Love has already found you.* Right here, right now, there is Love. Love, in every season.

Even when you've yet to find love, may your eyes be opened to the reality that *Love has already found you.*

Reflection Questions for Couples

1. "Trusting God goes hand in hand with the choices we make on a daily basis, and those choices will either lead us toward love or push us away from love." As you reflect on this statement, ask yourself if there are any steps you can take that will move you toward a deeper love and a healthier relationship.

2. What harmful things in your personal life might God be trying to eliminate in the season of winter?

3. In what ways has God's love been revealed to you in this particular season?

Reflection Questions for Singles

1. "Trusting God goes hand in hand with the choices we make on a daily basis, and those choices will either lead us toward love or push us away from love." As you reflect on this statement, ask yourself if there are any action steps you can take that will move you toward love and healthy relationships.

2. What harmful things in your personal life might God be trying to eliminate in the season of winter?

3. In what ways has God's love been revealed to you in this particular season?

NOTES

Chapter 1: Spring Is in the Air—Planting Good Seeds

1. Warren Wiersbe, *The Bible Exposition Commentary: New Testament, Volume I* (Colorado Springs, CO: Victor, 2001).

2. In my book *Choosing Marriage* (Eugene, OR: Harvest House, 2018), I lay out the specific choices you can make today in order to build a better marriage for tomorrow. There are many things you can do to increase your intimacy, strengthen your communication, build your faith, take down your walls, nurture your sex life, and engage in productive conflict.

Chapter 2: What's Bloomin'—The Laws of Attraction

1. Judy Scheel, "Culture Dictates the Standard of Beauty," *PsychologyToday.com*, April 24, 2014, https://www.psychologytoday.com/us/blog/when-food-is-family/201404/culture-dictates-the -standard-beauty.

2. Amber Petty, "How Women's Perfect Body Type Changed Throughout History," *TheList.com*, https://www.thelist.com/44261/womens-perfect-body-types-changed-throughout-history.

3. C.G. Jung, *Psychological Types*, The Collected Works of C.J. Jung, vol. 6 (Princeton, NJ: Princeton University Press, 1976). Originally published in 1921. Available online at https://www .jungiananalysts.org.uk/wp-content/uploads/2018/07/C.-G.-Jung-Collected-Works-Volume -6_-Psychological-Types.pdf.

4. The Myers and Briggs Foundation, *MBTI Basics*, https://www.myersbriggs.org/my-mbti-person ality-type/mbti-basics/home.htm?bhcp=1.

5. Debra Fileta, "How Much Do Looks Matter? The Response Will Shock You," October 8, 2016, *TrueLoveDates.com*, https://truelovedates.com/how-much-do-looks-matter-the-responses-will -shock-you.

6. For a deeper conversation on majors and minors, see chapter 5, "Do You Know What You Want?" from my book *True Love Dates* (Grand Rapids, MI: Zondervan, 2013).

7. For more on dating inward, see section 1 of *True Love Dates*.

8. Debra Fileta, *Choosing Marriage* (Eugene, OR: Harvest House, 2018), 63.

Chapter 4: Warmth—The Bond of Emotional Connection

1. Charles Q. Choi, "Itsy Bitsy Spider's Web 10 Times Stronger Than Kevlar," *LiveScience.com*, September 24, 2010, https://www.livescience.com/8686-itsy-bitsy-spider-web-10-times-stronger -kevlar.html.

2. *Spider Silk Is Stronger Than Steel—And Now It Can Be Made in a Lab*, NPR.com, January 14, 2017, https://www.npr.org/2017/01/14/509807212/spider-silk-is-stronger-than-steel-and-now-it -can-be-made-in-a-lab.

3. Liz Higgins, *Marriage Is Not a Big Thing, It's a Million Little Things*, The Gottman Relationship Blog, July 24, 2017, https://www.gottman.com/blog/marriage-not-big-thing-million-little-things.

4. John Gottman, *The Relationship Cure: A 5 Step Guide to Strengthening Your Marriage, Family, and Friendships* (New York: Harmony Books, 2001), 4.

5. David Naugle, Dallas Baptist University, *The Biblical Conception of the "Heart,"* 2001 Summer Institute in Christian Scholarship, July 11, 2001, https://www3.dbu.edu/naugle/pdf/institute_handouts/general/biblical_heart.pdf.

6. Debra Fileta, *Choosing Marriage* (Eugene, OR: Harvest House, 2018), 64.

7. Mekahlo Medina and Jonathan Lloyd, "Turned Down by Kate Upton, Teen Has 'Surreal' Prom Date with Supermodel," *NBC.com*, May 24, 2013, https://www.nbclosangeles.com/news/local/Nina-Agdal-Kate-Upton-Jake-Davison-Supermodel-Prom-Sports-Illustrated-Carls-Jr-208820251.html.

8. C.S. Lewis, *The Four Loves* (New York: Harcourt, Brace, 1960), 121.

Chapter 5: Heat—Sexual Connection

1. P. Roger Hillerstrom, *Intimate Deception: Escaping the Trap of Sexual Impurity* (Sisters, OR: Multnomah, 1988).

2. Debra Fileta, *Choosing Marriage* (Eugene, OR: Harvest House, 2018). See also Kevin Lehman, *Sheet Music: Uncovering the Secrets of Sexual Intimacy in Marriage* (Carol Stream, IL: Tyndale House, 2003).

Chapter 6: Fire—Spiritual Intimacy

1. E.L. Lehrer and C.U. Chiswick, *Religion as a Determinant of Marital Stability*, C.U. Demography (1993), 30:385, https://doi.org/10.2307/2061647.

2. Annette Mahoney, Kenneth I. Pargament, Tracy Jewell, Aaron B. Swank, Eric Scott, Erin Emery, Mark Rye, "Marriage and the spiritual realm: The role of proximal and distal religious constructs in marital functioning," *Journal of Family Psychology* 13, no. 3 (September 1999), 21-38.

Chapter 7: Goodbye, Green—The Colors of Compatibility

1. "Money Ruining Marriages in America: A Ramsey Solutions Study," *www.DaveRamsey.com*, https://www.daveramsey.com/pr/money-ruining-marriages-in-america.

Chapter 8: Vibrant Colors—Conflict Is Key

1. John Gottman, *The Seven Principles for Making Marriage Work: A Practical Guide from the Country's Foremost Relationship Expert* (New York: Three Rivers Press, 1999), 129-30.

2. Gottman, *The Seven Principles*, 131.

3. Kel Holliday, *Getting to Know Your Conflict Style*, TransformGroup.com, November 18, 2014, https://www.transformgroup.com.au/getting-to-know-your-conflict-style/.

4. Irvin Yalom, *The Gift of Therapy* (New York: Harper Perennial, 2002), 17-18.

5. Debra Fileta, *Choosing Marriage* (Eugene, OR: Harvest House, 2018), 70.

Chapter 9: Bare Branches—Dropping the Cover

1. Robert S. Feldman, James A. Forrest, Benjamin R. Happ, "Self-Presentation and Verbal Deception: Do Self-Presenters Lie More?" *Basic and Applied Social Psychology* 24, no. 2, (2002), 163-70, https://pdfs.semanticscholar.org/3afb/29f9ca3abdd784704bde06265742ec 7b0b3a.pdf.

Chapter 10: Frost—The Chill of Apathy

1. Isabelle Pittaway, "Frosts Wipe Out 80 Per Cent of Victorian Grower's Wildflower Crop," *ABC*

Rural, August 8, 2017, https://www.abc.net.au/news/rural/2017-08-09/frost-destroys-victorian-wildflower-crop/8785928.

2. Frost Destroys Victorian Crops, *Facebook.com*, November 15, 2017, https://www.facebook.com/ABCRural/videos/frost-destroys-victorian-crops/1498443020204921/.

Chapter 11: Freeze—Stuck in Love

1. Jill Mahoney, "Hockey-Arena Greenhouse a Northern Oasis", *TheGlobeandMail.com*, April 21, 2018, https://www.theglobeandmail.com/news/national/hockey-arena-greenhouse-a-northern-oasis/article1138066/.

2. Gary Chapman, *The Five Love Languages: The Secret to Love That Lasts* (Chicago: Northfield Publishing, 1995).

Chapter 12: The Thaw—Spring Will Come Again

1. Matthew Kronsberg, "Why Farmers Want Cold Winters," *Grist.org*, February 16, 2012, https://grist.org/sustainable-farming/why-farms-want-cold-winters/.

2. Ibid.

Acknowledgments

Writing a book is truly a labor of love, but it's not a labor that you can do alone. Behind the scenes of every meaningful book, there is a team of family, friends, colleagues, editors, and an entire tribe of people who believe in you and the message God has called you to proclaim through words on a page. I am grateful for my tribe and for their voices cheering me on every step of the way. I am fully aware that without them this project would still be a dream.

To my husband, John: my partner, my love, my best friend, and my number one fan. We are a team in every sense of the word. Just you and me, baby. Thank you for your constant love and support. Thank you for everything you see in me and for giving me what I need to shine brightly in the place God has called me to shine. But more so, thank you for the way you honor and love me behind the scenes. Our love is the *reason* I love the subject of marriage.

To Ella, Eli, and Ezzy: Thank you for encouraging Mommy to do what God has called me to do. Thank you for your many book title ideas, and for your zeal in wanting to read all my books even before you're old enough to be allowed to. One day, I pray that these words will bless, shape, and encourage you to pursue love in a way that honors God. I love you so much.

To my entire Harvest House family: I'll never forget how you loaded up and squeezed into a 15-passanger van, road-tripping to come and meet me for the first time at my speaking engagement. You sat in the front row with big smiles, cheering me on. I knew then what I know now: This was not a partnership; this was family. To Kathleen, Jessica, and Sherrie: Working so closely with you is truly a joy and an honor. To my literary agent and friend, Don Jacobson: Thank you for always believing in me and seeing beyond what I could see.

To my entire tribe of friends, followers, podcast listeners, and community of readers at *TrueLoveDates.com*: Your support is invaluable. Every e-mail, every message, and every encouragement has been used by God to fuel the work that He has called me to do. I cherish every single one of you, and I thank God every day for the privilege it is to serve and lead you in the subject of relationships. Thank you for inviting me into your lives and for entrusting me with your hearts. I will never take that privilege for granted.

And to the only One who holds all things together: my Lord and my God. How undeserving I am to have the honor of bringing this message to the people You love. Thank You for trusting me with this important work. Thank You for guiding me, and teaching me, and pouring into me with every single word on the page through Your Holy Spirit. May these words be an offering to You, the true Lover of my soul.

About the Author

Debra Fileta is a licensed professional counselor, national speaker, relationship expert, and the author of *True Love Dates* and *Choosing Marriage*. She's also the creator of the popular relationship advice blog *TrueLoveDates.com*, as well as the *Love + Relationships* podcast, reaching millions of people with the message that healthy people make healthy relationships. Debra and her husband, John, have been joyfully married for more than a decade and have three beautiful children. Connect with her on Facebook or Instagram @TrueLoveDates.

www.TrueLoveDates.com

Also from Debra Fileta...*Choosing Marriage*

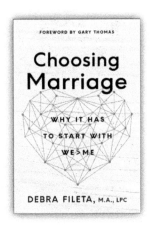

Is Marriage Worth It?

Many couples say "I do" with a combination of high hopes and fairy tale fantasies—but there's a difference between the expectations of marriage and the reality of it. Whether you're married, single, or dating, now is the time to ask yourself: *What steps can I take today to build an incredible marriage for tomorrow?*

With compassion and clarity, licensed counselor and relationship expert Debra Fileta shows that when we can work through the struggles of marriage, we get to experience the joys! Learn about eight powerful choices that will encourage and equip you to take your marriage from *average* to *exceptional* and find astonishing survey results from thousands of singles and couples on topics like love and attraction, sex, conflict, and communication.

A beautiful exchange occurs when you learn what it means to choose *we* before *me*. Discover practical steps that will give you confidence and courage on the adventure of *Choosing Marriage*.

Printed in the USA
CPSIA information can be obtained
at www.ICGtesting.com
LVHW021136180923
758464LV00001B/83